PRELIMINARY INVENTORY
OF THE
RECORDS
OF

UNITED STATES ARMY COMMANDS

RECORD GROUP 98

COMPILED BY
Maizie Johnson

AND
Sarah Powell

HERITAGE BOOKS
2011

HERITAGE BOOKS

AN IMPRINT OF HERITAGE BOOKS, INC.

Books, CDs, and more—Worldwide

For our listing of thousands of titles see our website
at
www.HeritageBooks.com

A Facsimile Reprint
Published 2011 by
HERITAGE BOOKS, INC.
Publishing Division
100 Railroad Ave. #104
Westminster, Maryland 21157

Originally published
The National Archives
National Archives and Records Service
General Services Administration
Washington: 1966

International Standard Book Numbers
Paperbound: 978-0-7884-3478-5
Clothbound: 978-0-7884-8669-2

CONTENTS

Appendix:

INTRODUCTION

History

The Revolutionary Army was disbanded November 5, 1783, in accordance with a proclamation of Congress of October 18, 1783. In the belief that standing armies in time of peace were "inconsistent with the principles of republican governments, dangerous to the liberties of a free people, and generally converted into destructive engines for establishing despotism," Congress, on May 26, 1784, resolved that western posts should be garrisoned by State militia or by the use of the Continental troops then at West Point. To implement this belief, Congress, in its resolution of June 2, 1784, directed that all troops--including all officers above the rank of captain--in the service of the United States be discharged, except 25 privates to guard stores at Fort Pitt and 55 privates to guard stores at West Point and other magazines. Thus Henry Knox, Brigadier General of Artillery, who had served as commander in chief since the resignation of George Washington on December 23, 1783, was honorably discharged, and the position of commander in chief was abolished. Also discharged were all officers of the First American Regiment of Infantry, located at Fort Pitt, under the command of Col. Henry Jackson.

In the summer of 1784 the Army of the United States consisted of the First Regiment of Infantry, organized by a resolution of June 3, 1784, under the command of Lt. Col. Josiah Harmar. The artillery company, under Capt. John Doughty, which had been retained in the service, formed part of this new infantry regiment. As the commander of the single unit of the Army, Colonel Harmar in effect commanded the Army. On July 31, 1787, Harmar was breveted brigadier general and placed on duty as general in chief of the Army consisting of less than 600 men, thus commanding not only his own regiment but also the battalion of U.S. artillery that was organized under a resolution of October 20, 1786, and that consisted of four companies under Doughty, now a major.

With Miami Indian troubles on the northwest frontier, Congress, in an act of March 3, 1791, empowered the President to add another infantry regiment and provide for further protection of the frontiers. Accordingly, Gov. Arthur St. Clair, of the Northwest Territory, was appointed major general, thus superseding Harmar as general in chief, and the 2d Regiment of Infantry was organized. Upon the resignation of St. Clair, on March 5, 1792, Anthony Wayne was appointed major general and succeeded St. Clair as general in chief, under provisions of an act of the same day. By virtue of the same act, March 5, 1792, the Army of the United States was designated as the Legion of the United States on September 4, 1792.

The organization of the Army as a Legion lasted only four years, until November 1, 1796. Although three additional infantry regiments had been authorized, only two more were actually organized, making a total of four. Each of four sublegions of the Legion was composed of one infantry regiment, one troop of dragoons, and one of the four artillery companies that formerly made up the battalion of artillery. When the Legion organization was disbanded in 1796, pursuant to an act of May 30, 1796, the infantry in the first two sublegions resumed their former designations of 1st and 2d Regiments of Infantry. The infantry of the 3d and 4th sublegions became the 3d and 4th Regiments of Infantry, r spectively. The four artillery companies were incorporated into the Corps of Artillerists and Engineers, which had been authorized by an act of May 9, 1794, as a unit separate from the Legion; and the two troops of dragoons that were retained in service after the disbandment of the Legion, with no field officer, later became part of the Regiment of Light Dragoons authorized by an act of July 16, 1798. In December 1796 Major General Wayne died, and his second in command, Brig. Gen. James Wilkinson, became general in chief.

Alarmed by the possibility of war with France, Congress, by an act of April 27, 1798, provided for a second regiment of artillerists and engineers and, by an act of the following July 16, for 12 additional infantry regiments, a "commander of the army" with the rank of lieutenant general, three additional generals, and the aforementioned Regiment of Light Dragoons. George Washington was appointed lieutenant general but never was called into the field, and Congress abolished that rank by an act of March 3, 1799. Henry Knox having declined a general's commission, only two additional generals were commissioned. They were Alexander Hamilton, to serve as Inspector General, and Charles C. Pinckney. Both were commissioned as major generals on July 19, 1798. For the first time, the field establishments were divided into two commands, those of Pinckney and Wilkinson, both independent commands responsible to the Secretary of War. Pinckney's district comprised the posts and forts in Georgia, Tennessee, North Carolina, South Carolina, and Virginia, and at Carlisle, Pa. Wilkinson commanded the remaining installations.

In 1800, with the French threat diminishing, retrenchment set in. By an act of May 14 of that year, the Army was reduced by the 12 infantry regiments and the Regiment of Light Dragoons authorized two years earlier to four regiments of infantry, and all officers commissioned by the July 1798 act were discharged. Pinckney's command was abolished and Brigadier General Wilkinson once again became general in chief of the Army, which now consisted of two regiments of artillerists and engineers and the four regiments of infantry. Two of the latter were abolished in 1802. Also in 1802 a Regiment of Artillerists was formed from the two regiments of artillerists and engineers. (At the same time, a Corps of Engineers was established to be stationed at West Point and to "constitute a Military Academy.")

Meanwhile Wilkinson remained general in chief and divided his command into 11 districts. Some of these districts had been previously established as early as 1798 or 1799. Late in 1800, when Wilkinson moved his headquarters from Washington to the western frontier, the districts on the seaboard and on the frontier of Georgia were placed under the jurisdiction of Lt. Col. Henry Burbeck. And again, in 1805, when Wilkinson moved his headquarters to St. Louis, he established two departments--his own, west of the Appalachians to include New Orleans and the Territory of Louisiana, and Colonel Burbeck's, east of the mountains with headquarters at Fort McHenry. Burbeck, as chief of a department, acted independently of Wilkinson and thus was immediately responsible to the Secretary of War. The district organization was continued throughout the period, but some changes were made in district areas as new forts were garrisoned or seacoast defenses were added.

Alarmed once again by the possibility of war, this time with Great Britain, Congress in 1808 authorized the raising of additional forces. By an act of April 12, 1808, Congress authorized a Regiment of Light Artillery, a Regiment of Light Dragoons, five additional infantry regiments (Nos. 3-7), and a Regiment of Riflemen, as well as the commissioning of two additional brigadier generals. On February 15, 1809, Wade Hampton and Peter Gansevoort were commissioned as brigadier generals, and the United States was divided into three districts, whose commanders were to exercise independent control, each being directly responsible to the War Department. The Northern District, comprising the country north of the Potomac, was placed under the command of Gansevoort, with headquarters at Albany. Hampton commanded the Southern District, and Brigadier General Wilkinson took the Western District, often referred to as the District of Mississippi. The former districts were retained, a few of which were now referred to as subdistricts. From the time that Wilkinson returned to Washington in June 1810 until July 1812, after his court-martial and acquittal, Hampton exercised command over both the Southern and the Western Districts as the Southern Department, with headquarters at Charleston, S.C. The Northern District became the Northern Department and on January 27, 1812, Henry Dearborn was appointed the senior major general of the Army and was assigned to the command of this department, with headquarters at Albany.

Less than six months before war was declared on Great Britain, Congress authorized, by an act of January 11, 1812, an additional 10 regiments of infantry (Nos. 8-17), two additional regiments of artillery (Nos. 2 and 3), and one more regiment of light dragoons (No. 2). On June 26, one week after the declaration of war, Congress authorized an additional eight infantry regiments (Nos. 18-25). On January 29, 1813, it authorized 19 more infantry regiments (Nos. 26-44); on February 10, 1814, three more rifle regiments (Nos. 2-4); and on March 30, 1814, four more infantry regiments (Nos. 45-48) and the consolidation of three regiments of artillery into a Corps of Artillery, which was formed on May 12, 1814.

Upon the signing of the peace treaty at Ghent on December 24, 1814, President Madison and Congress faced decisions with regard to a military peacetime establishment. Under an act of March 3, 1815, the infantry was completely reorganized and reduced to eight regiments; the four rifle regiments were consolidated into one regiment; and the remaining regiment of dragoons (the two having been merged with the first by an act of March 30, 1814) was merged with the Corps of Artillery. By an act of March 2, 1821, the eight regiments of infantry were reduced to seven; the rifle regiment was discharged; and the three regiments of artillery forming the Corps of Artillery were merged with the Regiment of Light Artille y to form a Corps of Artillery with four regiments.

With an increase in the Army during the War of 1812 of about 25,000 men over the previous maximum of 5,500 men, it was necessary that the War Department be reorganized in order to relieve the Secretary of War from some of his burden. By an act of March 3, 1813, Congress authorized the Secretary of War to prepare regulations better defining and prescribing the duties of the officers of the bureaus as well as those of the general and regimental staff. As a consequence, by a War Department General Order of March 19, 1813, the United States was divided into nine military districts, later increased to ten on July 2, 1814. These were each independent commands, whose commanders reported directly to the War Department. As mentioned before, the United States had upon occasion been divided into commands, but in 1813 the organization of the Army of the United States and its field stations on a geographical command basis became a permanent concept.

On May 17, 1815, this particular geographical command organization was changed, and the United States was divided into a Division of the North and a Division of the South, with five military departments under each division. Again, in May 1821, the organization was changed and the United States was divided into Eastern and Western Departments. Although the areas of commands and the names of commands afterwards changed periodically, especially during the Civil War, the Army has not again been controlled directly by one commander in chief or as a single command under the Secretary of War.

General Description of the Records Covered

The records described in this inventory are those of Record Group 98, Records of the United States Army Commands, for the period 1784-1821.

They are the records of the field establishments of the Army and include the records of divisions, departments, districts, expeditions, posts, and units of the Army. Most of the records described here were in the custody of the Adjutant General's Office (AGO) until they were transferred to the National Archives. The year 1821 has been selected as the concluding date for this inventory because it was the year used by the AGO in separating the records of discontinued commands for the post-Revolutionary War period from those of the pre-Civil War and Civil War period. Records after 1821 will be described in several separate inventories.

In an attempt to facilitate the use and inventorying of records accessioned from the AGO, the National Archives established Record Group 98 for the records of discontinued commands of the Army as opposed to the records of the AGO itself relating to them. While the records of discontinued commands were in the custody of the AGO, many changes were made in their arrangement, especially in the loose records. This inventory describes bound volumes only, and especially the larger part of a set of bound volumes that were put together, indexed, numbered, added to, and renumbered by the AGO. This set of 689 numbered volumes is referred to in entry 2 of the inventory and is listed in the appendix to it. The disposition, when known, of those volumes in the set that are not described in the inventory is also shown. At the end of the list of numbered volumes is a list of 27 unnumbered volumes received by the National Archives that are also described in the inventory. Some extant volumes relating to this period were never deposited with the AGO and may be found in libraries or other depositories throughout the United States.

The loose records relating to the bound records described here were incorporated by the AGO into its own office records and are described in Preliminary Inventory No. 17, which describes records in Record Group 94, Records of The Adjutant General's Office. For example, the "letters received" by the AGO described in entry 12 of Preliminary Inventory No. 17 are not only letters received by the AGO but also other letters that the AGO had and decided to file with them.

Definitions

Most of the entries in this inventory describe orderly books and company books, for these were the titles used for the two main books kept by each office or unit.

An orderly book contains orders received from superior commands as well as those issued. The typical company orderly book will therefore contain War Department General Orders; division, department, and district orders; and regimental and garrison orders both received and issued. Many unexpected items of information may be found in them. For example, volume 370/253, Orderly Book for an Unidentified Company, 7th Infantry, 1812 (described in entry 184), in addition to the usual and routine orders, contains the following:

1. General order, February 2, 1812, of brigade inspector to Brig. Gen. Wade Hampton, announcing the disposition of troops within Hampton's department.

2. Order, January 9, 1812, Inspector's Office, Washington, announcing promotions in the U.S. Army.

3. Order, February 19, 1812, Inspector's Office, Washington, announcing the charges and specifications and proceedings of the general court-martial presided over by Brig. Gen. Peter Gansevoort in the case of Brig. Gen. James Wilkinson, September-December 1811; the decision of acquittal; and President Madison's approval of Wilkinson's acquittal.

4. General order, May 9, 1812, of Brig. Gen. Wade Hampton, publishing proceedings of the court-martial presided over by Col. Leonard Covington in the case of Col. Thomas Cushing, 2d Infantry, for charges and specifications preferred by General Hampton.

5. District orders of Col. Joseph Constant, in charge of the troops and garrisons within the Territories of Orleans and Mississippi, including West Florida.

6. Order, July 15, 1812, of Brig. Gen. James Wilkinson, announcing his resumption of command of the District of Mississippi.

7. Order, July 13, 1812, of War Department, announcing the appointment of Col. Alexander Smyth, rifle regiment, as Inspector General of the Army with the rank of brigadier general.

8. Order, July 14, 1812, of the Adjutant General's Office, Washington, announcing the appointment of Col. Thomas Cushing as Adjutant General of the Army with the rank of brigadier general.

9. Extract of order, June 20, 1809, of Brig. Gen. Peter Gansevoort, announcing his assumption of command of the Northern District with headquarters at Albany.

10. Letter, December 18, 1810, from Brig. Gen. Wade Hampton to Col. Alexander Smyth, Rifle Corps, informing him of the extent of his command.

A company book may contain all or any of the following: Registers of commissioned officers, noncommissioned officers, men transferred out, men transferred in, deaths, desertions, men fined by court-martial, men discharged, men furloughed, and men in captivity; descriptive lists of officers and enlisted men; clothing accounts; accounts of arms and ammunition; and accounts of camp equipage and stationery.

Identification of Records

In most cases there is no known method of identifying positively the ownership of orderly books. Companies seldom issued orders, and all companies copied all the orders they received into their orderly books, as did adjutants and inspectors. Consequently, if all companies of a regiment were at the same post, all company orderly books of that regiment generally duplicated each other. In the belief that the searcher would be aided by having these orderly books grouped in series, even if incorrectly identified, an attempt has been made to assign these books to companies by name when a reasonable choice of name could be made. Names on covers, inserted records peculiar to one company, and known locations of particular companies have been used as guides, and then such tentatively identified books have been placed with others when a sequence was apparent. At times the only recourse was to assign a book of a series of books to an "unidentified" company. This method of identification, although no guarantee of accuracy, should not impose an impossible burden on the searcher in view of the vast amount of duplication. Orderly books that were not completely duplicated are those of companies detailed from the main regiment. In such instances the location of the detail has been noted in the entry.

Organization of the Inventory

This inventory has been organized in two sections: (1) The geographical commands and (2) the units of the Army. The entries for the geographical commands have been arranged in three periodic groups: (1) The period 1784-1813, when the geographical command structure was less precise and for which the National Archives has only a few records; (2) the period March 1813-May 1815, when the United States was divided into nine (or ten) military departments; and (3) the period May 1815-May 1821, when the United States was divided into two divisions and thereunder into departments.

Each unit of the Army was under the jurisdiction of the same geographical command as was the post at which the unit was stationed. Because the frequent transfer of units from post to post placed them under different superior commands periodically, the entries for the units have been arranged alphabetically by type of unit only, and thereunder numerically by regiment number (if applicable), with no reference to a superior command. In many cases there have been several regiments having the same number over the years. The dates for the existence of a given regiment for which there are records are in parentheses after the number of the regiment, and the dates of the records inventoried follow the complete name; for example, 2d (1791-1815) Regiment, 1802-1⁻

Related Record Groups

Other records in the National Archives relating to U.S. Army commands are in Record Group 94, Records of The Adjutant General's Office, and Record Group 107, Records of the Secretary of War.

Bibliography

Thomas H. S. Hamersly, comp., Army Register of the United States, 1779-1879 (Washington, 1880).

Francis B. Heitman, Historical Register and Dictionary of the U.S. Army, 1789-1903 (Washington, 1903. 2 vols).

James Ripley Jacobs, The Beginning of the U.S. Army, 1783-1812 (Princeton, 1947).

Walter Lowrie and Matthew St. Clair Clarke, eds., American State Papers, Class V, Military Affairs, Vol. 1, 1789-1819 (Washington, 1832).

Theophilus F. Rodenbough and William L. Haskin, eds., The Army of the United States (New York, 1896).

Raphael P. Thian, comp., Legislative History of the General Staff of the United States. . . From 1775 to 1901 (Washington, 1901).

Raphael P. Thian, comp., Notes Illustrating the Military Geography of the United States . . . 1813-80 (Washington, 1881).

I N V E N T O R Y

RECORDS OF UNITED STATES ARMY COMMANDS
1784-1821

I. Finding Aids to Records

The two finding aids described in entries 1 and 2 contain references to volume numbers cited in the entries that follow. The first number of a pair separated by a diagonal (like 402/286) is the "new" volume number used in series 2, and the second number is the "old" volume number used in series 1.

NAME INDEX TO 535 VOLUMES OF RECORDS (1784-1821) MAINLY OF U.S. ARMY
    COMMANDS. n.d. 1.vol. 4 in.   1
    Arranged by type of unit and thereunder numerically by regiment number. Contains an alphabetical name index and also a table converting the "old" numbers used for the 535 volumes to "new" volume numbers assigned later when the set was increased to 689 volumes and renumbered. The table is arranged numerically by the "old" volume number.

NUMERICAL LIST OF 689 VOLUMES OF RECORDS (1784-1821) MAINLY OF U.S.
    ARMY COMMANDS. n.d. 1 vol. 1/2 in.   2
    List of volumes as renumbered by AGO. The list is reproduced in the appendix. The volume also contains a location register of unbound records. Compiled before May 1874.

II. Records of Departments, Districts, Divisions, and Posts

A. Records Relating Mainly to the 1784-1813 Period

1. Departments, Districts, and Expeditions

a. Troops on the Mississippi, 1799-1800

Maj. Thomas Cushing functioned as adjutant to Brig. Gen. James Wilkinson. In 1800 Cushing was stationed in the City of Washington as Inspector for the Army. For a continuation of his letters sent, see entry 1 of Preliminary Inventory No. 17, Records of The Adjutant General's Office.

LETTERS SENT BY MAJ. THOMAS CUSHING, COMMANDING TROOPS ON THE MISSIS-
    SIPPI. July 1799-Mar. 1800. 1 vol. (No. 402/286). 1/2 in.   3
    Arranged chronologically. Name and subject index.

LETTERS RECEIVED BY MAJ. THOMAS CUSHING, COMMANDING TROOPS ON THE MIS-
SISSIPPI. Apr.-Nov. 1799. 1 vol. (No. 401/285). 1/2 in.   4
Arranged chronologically. Name and subject index.

b. District of Maj. Gen. Charles C. Pinckney, 1800

ORDERLY BOOK OF THE DEPUTY ADJUTANT GENERAL TO THE DISTRICT COMMANDER,
MAJ. GEN. CHARLES C. PINCKNEY. Apr.-June 1800. 1 vol. (No. 383/
267). 1/2 in.   5
Arranged chronologically.

c. Southern Department, 1812-13

GENERAL ORDERS RECEIVED AND ORDERS ISSUED BY THE SOUTHERN DEPARTMENT,
CHARLESTON, S.C. June 1812-Feb. 1813. 2 vols. (No. 678/-; 677/-).
2 in.   6
Arranged chronologically. Subject index in second volume.

d. Northern Department, 1812-13

ORDERLY BOOK FOR THE ASSISTANT INSPECTOR GENERAL, NORTHERN DEPARTMENT.
Sept. 1812-Feb. 1813. 1 vol. (No. 447/345). 1 in.   7
Arranged chronologically. Name index. Also contains: (1) List of
deserters from the British Army, Sept. 1814, at Plattsburg; (2) register of Army officers, Apr. 1813, which predates the one of the same
year in Hamersly's Army Register; and (3) orders announcing details
issued by the Adjutant General, Fort George, May-June 1813.

e. Sabine Expedition, 1806-7

ORDERS AND MUSTER REPORTS OF THE SABINE EXPEDITION. 1806-7. 1 vol.
(No. 386/270). 1/2 in.   8
Arranged by type of record.

2. Posts

a. Castle Island (Fort Independence), Boston Harbor,
1786-87; 1803-15

ORDERLY BOOK FOR THE GARRISON AT CASTLE ISLAND, BOSTON HARBOR.
1786-87. 1 vol. 1/2 in.   9
Arranged chronologically.

RECORDS OF THE GARRISON AT FORT INDEPENDENCE, BOSTON HARBOR ("CASTLE
    ISLAND RECORDS"). 1803-15. 1 vol. 4 in.   10
    Arranged chronologically. Contains General Orders and division
orders received, and garrison orders issued; also letters sent and
received. Contains historical information relating to Fort Independence before 1803.

LETTERS RECEIVED AND SENT, DISTRICT AND GENERAL ORDERS RECEIVED, AND
    DETACHMENT ORDERS ISSUED BY COL. JOHN BRECK, COMMANDING.
    Feb.-Mar. 1815. 1 vol. (No. 366/-). 1/2 in.   11
    Arranged chronologically.

b. Fort Johnston, N.C., 1795-1811

ORDERLY BOOK FOR THE GARRISON AT FORT JOHNSTON, N.C. 1795-1811.
    1 vol. 3 in.   12
    Arranged generally chronologically. Contains a few letters
received.

c. Garrison at New Orleans, 1806-16

ORDERLY BOOKS OF THE ADJUTANT OF THE GARRISON OF NEW ORLEANS, UNDER
    THE COMMAND OF MAJ. WILLIAM MacREA   Jan.-Dec. 1806; June 1807-
    Mar. 1809. 4 vols. (Nos. 487/388; 368/234; 472/372; 437/334).
    4 in.   13
    Arranged chronologically. Name index in volume 437. Contains
War Department and Gen. James Wilkinson's General Orders, district
orders, and garrison orders. Also contains orderly books of a detachment, later called battalion, under command of Maj. Z. M. Pike,
consisting of the Companies of Davis and Bentley, 6th Infantry; Cut-
ler's Company, of the 7th Infantry; and the late Lott's Company, of
the 6th Infantry, Mar.-Aug. 1809. This battalion moved from New
Orleans to Camp Terre au Boeuf in June 1809.

ORDERLY BOOKS OF THE ADJUTANT OF THE GARRISON OF NEW ORLEANS, UNDER
    THE COMMAND OF MAJ. WILLIAM MacREA AND MAJ. GEORGE GIBSON.
    Nov. 1810-Jan. 1813. 2 vols. (Nos. 488/389; 369/236). 3 in.   14
    Arranged chronologically. Contains War Department and Gen. James
Wilkinson's General Orders, district orders, and garrison orders.
MacRea was in the 1st Regiment of Artillerists, and Gibson was in the
7th Infantry Regiment.

PROVISION RETURNS. Apr. 1809-Jan. 1816. 1 vol. (No. 360/420). 1 in. 15
    Arranged chronologically. The garrison troops were composed
chiefly, but not entirely, of companies from the 3d Infantry Regiment to May 1815, and thereafter from the 1st Infantry Regiment, and
were stationed at New Orleans or nearby Fort Jackson, Bayou St. John,
and Pass Christian.

3. Miscellaneous, 1795

GUARD DETAILS AND ROSTERS OF OFFICERS. 1795. 1 vol. 1/2 in. 16
   Arranged by type of record and thereunder chronologically.

B. Records Relating Mainly to the 1813-15 Period

1. 1st Military District, 1813-15

It consisted of the States of Massachusetts and New Hampshire and was commanded by Brig. Gen. Thomas H. Cushing and Maj. Gen. Henry Dearborn. It was merged into the 2d Military Department in 1815.

REGISTER OF MEN FURLOUGHED AND DISCHARGED AND A LIST OF OFFICERS IN THE
   DISTRICT. 1813-15. 1 vol. (No. 569/-). 1 in. 17
   Arranged by type of record.

2. 2d Military District, 1814-15

It consisted of the States of Rhode Island and Connecticut with headquarters at New London, Conn., and at Providence, R.I. It was commanded by Brig. Gen. Henry Burbeck and Brig. Gen. Thomas H. Cushing. It was merged into the 2d Military Department in 1815.

GENERAL ORDERS RECEIVED AND DISTRICT ORDERS ISSUED. June 1814-July
   1815. 1 vol. (No. 127/-). 1 in. 18
   Arranged chronologically.

3. 3d Military District, 1812-19

It consisted of the State of New York, from the sea to the Highlands, and the State of New Jersey, with headquarters at New York. It was commanded by Brig. Gen. George Izard, Brig. Gen. Moses Porter, Brig. Gen. Henry Dearborn, Gov. Daniel D. Tompkins of New York, and Brig. Gen. John P. Boyd. It was merged into the 3d and 4th Military Departments in 1815.

Records extending beyond May 1815 are the records of the 3d Military Department.

LETTERS AND EXTRACTS OF LETTERS RECEIVED BY DANIEL D. TOMPKINS, GOV-
   ERNOR OF NEW YORK. 1812-14. 1 vol. 2 in. 19
   Arranged chronologically. Contains letters received from the War
Department and generals in the Northern Army.

ORDERLY BOOKS C. THE ADJUTANT GENERAL. June 1812-Sept. 1818. 4 vols.
 (Nos. 389/273; n.n.; 466/365; 449/347). 9 in.   20
 Arranged chronologically. From June 1812 until March 1813 these
are the records of the Commander of the Defense of the City and Harbor
of New York.

ORDERLY BOOKS OF THE INSPECTOR GENERAL. Mar. 1813-May 1815. 2 vols.
 (Nos. 458/357; 451/350). 3 in. Arranged chronologically.   21

GENERAL ORDERS ISSUED CONTAINING PROCEEDINGS OF GENERAL COURTS-MARTIAL.
 Nov. 1814-May 1818. 1 vol. (No. 461/360). 2 in.   22
 Arranged chronologically.

LIST OF OFFICERS REPORTING. Nov.1813-Apr. 1814. 1 vol. (No. 423/310).
 1 in.   23
 Arranged chronologically.

REGISTERS OF MEN DISCHARGED. 1813-19. 3 vols. (Nos. 553/-; 551/-;
 554/-). 3 in.   24
 Arranged by time period.

REGISTER OF MEN FURLOUGHED. Nov.1814-May 1815. 1 vol. (No. 40/322).
 1 in.   25
 Arranged chronologically.

COMPANY RETURNS RECEIVED BY THE INSPECTOR GENERAL. Jan.-Dec. 1814.
 1 vol. (No. 357/416). 1 in.   26
 Arranged chronologically.

RECEIPTS FOR BLANK FORMS ISSUED BY THE ADJUTANT GENERAL. Aug.-Oct.
 1814. 1 vol. (No. 514/417). 1/2 in.   27
 Arranged chronologically. Also contains receipts for paroles and
countersigns received from the Adjutant General by the various commanders at the harbor of New York under the 3d Military District, Apr. 1813-
Feb. 1815; arranged chronologically.

4. 4th Military District, 1813-19

It consisted of the States of Pennsylvania, from its eastern limits
to the Allegheny Mountains, and Delaware, with headquarters at Philadelphia. It was commanded by Brig. Gen. Joseph Bloomfield, Brig. Gen.
Edmund P. Gaines, Brig. Gen. Thomas Cadwallader, and Brig. Gen. Winfield
Scott. From about January to March 1815 General Scott commanded both
the 4th and 10th Military Districts from Baltimore, Md. In March he
moved his headquarters to Philadelphia. The 4th Military District was
merged into the 3d and 4th Departments in May 1815.

Records extending beyond May 1815 are those of the 4th Military Department.

LETTERS SENT, DISTRICT ORDERS ISSUED, AND GENERAL ORDERS RECEIVED.
   May 1813-Dec. 1814. 1 vol. (No. 393/276). 3 in.   <u>28</u>
   Arranged chronologically. Name and subject index.

ORDERLY BOOK. Nov.1814-June 1819. 1 vol. (No. 460/359). 1 in.   <u>29</u>
   Arranged chronologically. Contains General Orders and Division
orders received, and District and Department orders issued.

GENERAL ORDERS RECEIVED AND ISSUED BY THE ADJUTANT AND INSPECTOR GEN-
   ERAL OF THE 4TH AND 10TH MILITARY DISTRICTS. Jan.-Feb. 1815.
   1 vol. (No. 453/352). 1/2 in.   <u>30</u>
   Arranged chronologically.

REPORTS SENT BY THE INSPECTOR GENERAL OF THE 4TH AND 10TH MILITARY
   DISTRICTS.Jan.-Apr.1815.1 vol. (No. 358/418). 1 in.   <u>31</u>
   Arranged chronologically.

LISTS OF DISCHARGES, DESERTIONS, AND DEATHS. 1813-14. 1 vol. (No.563/-).
   1/2 in.   <u>32</u>
   Arranged by type of list.

5. <u>6th Military District, 1813-15</u>

It consisted of the States of North Carolina, South Carolina, and
Georgia, with headquarters at Charleston, S.C., and also at Fort Hawkins
and Milledgeville, Ga. It was commanded by Maj. Gen. Thomas Pinckney
and merged into the 6th and 7th Military Departments in 1815.

LETTERS SENT. Mar. 1813-June 1815. 2 vols. (Nos. 679/-; 675/-).
   3 in.   <u>33</u>
   Arranged chronologically. Name index in first volume (679). Volume 675 also contains various instructions to officers, 1812-14,
arranged chronologically.

ORDERLY BOOKS OF THE ADJUTANT GENERAL. Mar. 1813-Aug. 1814; Feb.-
   June 1815. 3 vols. (Nos. 682/-; 681/-; n.n.). 3 in.   <u>34</u>
   Arranged chronologically. Contains War Department General Orders,
district and daily orders, and Army regulations. Subject index to
first half (Mar.-Oct. 1813) of volume 682.

6. <u>7th Military District</u>

It consisted of the States of Tennessee and Louisiana and the Mississippi Territory, with headquarters at New Orleans, La., except for

the period July-Dec. 1814, when it was at various places in the field.
The district was commanded by Brig. Gen. Thomas Flournoy until June
1814 and thereafter by Maj. Gen. Andrew Jackson. It was merged into
the 8th and 9th Military Departments in 1815.

For records of the 7th Military District, see Division of the
South (II, C, 2) below.

7. 9th Military District and Northern Army, 1812-16

The district consisted of the States of Pennsylvania from the
Allegheny to the western limits, New York north of the Highlands, and
Vermont. The same general commanded both the district and the Northern
Army, and therefore headquarters of the district moved from place to
place as did headquarters of the Northern Army. The district was under
the following commanders: Maj. Gen. Henry Dearborn, Maj. Gen. James
Wilkinson, Bvt. Maj. Gen. Alexander Macomb, and Brig. Gen. George Izard.
It was merged into the 1st and 4th Military Departments in 1815.

a. Divisions (Wings), 1812-15

(1) Headquarters and 1st Division (Right Wing), 1813-15

LETTERS AND CIRCULARS SENT BY HEADQUARTERS AND THE RIGHT WING.
May 1814-June 1815. 1 vol. (No. 405/289). 1 in.   35
Arranged chronologically.

LETTERS SENT AND RECEIVED BY THE INSPECTOR GENERAL. May 1814-Feb.
1815. 1 vol. (No. 406/290). 1 in.   36
Arranged chronologically. Name index.

GENERAL ORDERS ISSUED BY MAJ. GEN. WADE HAMPTON. Apr.-Aug. 1813.
1 vol. (No. 495/396). 1/2 in.   37
Arranged chronologically. General Hampton was in command of the
5th Military District through May 1813, and became commander of the
Right Wing of the Northern Army at Burlington in July 1813.

GENERAL ORDERS ISSUED CONTAINING PROCEEDINGS OF GENERAL COURTS-MARTIAL.
July-Sept. 1814. 1 vol. (No. 455/354). 1 in.   38
Arranged chronologically.

ORDERS ISSUED BY THE ASSISTANT ADJUTANT AND THE INSPECTOR GENERAL
ANNOUNCING DETAILS. Mar.-Dec. 1814. 2 vols. (Nos.508/410;   39
509/411). 1 in.
Arranged chronologically.

ORDERLY BOOKS OF THE ADJUTANT GENERAL. Aug. 1813-June 1815. 4 vols.
   (Nos. 445/342; 442/339; 464/341; 465/364). 5 in.   <u>40</u>
   Arranged chronologically. Name and subject index in volume 442.

(2) <u>2d Division (Left Wing), 1812-15</u>

LETTERS AND ORDERS SENT BY GEN. EDMUND GAINES. Aug. 1814. 1 vol.
   (No. 512/414). 1 in.   <u>41</u>
   Arranged chronologically. Name index. Also contains guard details,
Aug.-Dec. 1814, arranged chronologically.

ORDERLY BOOK OF THE ADJUTANT AT SACKETT'S HARBOR. Sept. 1812-
   Sept. 1813. 1 vol. (No. 390/274). 2 in.   <u>42</u>
   Arranged chronologically. From Sept. 1812 to Jan. 1813 this is
the orderly book of Brig. Gen. Richard Dodge, commanding the 4th
Brigade of Detached Militia, and from Feb. to June 1813 the orderly
book of Col. Alexander E. Macomb, commanding the District of Oswego,
Sackett's Harbor, and Ogdensburg.

ORDERLY BOOKS OF THE ADJUTANT AT SACKETT'S HARBOR. Feb.-Nov. 1814;
   Feb.-June 1815. 3 vols. (Nos. 440/337; 446/343; 457/356). 4 in.   <u>43</u>
   Arranged chronologically, except for some overlap between the
first two volumes. Gen. Edmund Gaines and Col. G. E. Mitchell were
the post commanders. Contains orders issued by Right Wing, Northern
Army, and by Gaines after assuming command of the Army of the Niagara
Frontier.

ORDERLY BOOK OF THE INSPECTOR. Feb.-Mar. 1814; Sept. 1814-June 1815.
   1 vol. (No. 456/355). 1 in.   <u>44</u>
   Arranged chronologically. Inspector Josiah Snelling was an assistant inspector to Gen. Jacob Brown, 2d Division, until Jan. 1815, when
he took over the duties of Asst. Adj. John M. O'Connor under Col.
Cromwell Pearce, 1st Division.

ORDERS ISSUED BY THE ADJUTANT GENERAL AT SACKETT'S HARBOR ANNOUNCING
   DETAILS. July-Oct. 1813. 1 vol. (No. 507/409). 1 in.   <u>45</u>
   Arranged chronologically.

ORDERS ISSUED BY THE ASSISTANT ADJUTANT AT FRENCH MILLS ANNOUNCING
   DETAILS. Nov. 1813-Feb. 1814. 1 vol. (No. 396/279). 1/2 in.   <u>46</u>
   Arranged chronologically.

ORDERLY BOOK FOR THE SECOND BRIGADE. Aug.-Dec. 1813. 1 vol.
   (No. 506/408). 1 in.   <u>47</u>
   Arranged chronologically. Until about Oct. 1813 all infantry at
the post of Sackett's Harbor was in one brigade that consisted of
Regiments 9, 11, 14, 16, and 21. After that date the brigade was
called the Second Brigade and consisted of Regiments 5, 6, 15, and 22.

SECOND BRIGADE ORDERS ISSUED ANNOUNCING DETAILS. Aug.-Nov. 1813.
  1 vol. (No. 394/277). 1 in.   48
  Arranged chronologically. All infantry at the post of Sackett's
Harbor was in one brigade until about Oct. 1813, when it became known
as the Second Brigade. For additional records, see series 47.

FOURTH BRIGADE ORDERS ISSUED ANNOUNCING GUARD DETAILS. Oct.-Dec. 1813.
  1 vol. (No. 395/278). 1/2 in.   49
  Arranged chronologically. This Brigade was composed of Infantry
Regiments 9, 11, 14, 16, and 21.

BRIGADE ORDERS ISSUED ANNOUNCING DETAILS. May-July 1814. 1 vol.
  (No. 452/351). 1/2 in.   50
  Arranged chronologically. Brigade consisted of Infantry Regiments
9, 11, 22, and 25 under Bvt. Maj. Gerard D. Smith at Buffalo. In
early May 1814 this was General Scott's Brigade.

REGISTER OF MEN AND OFFICERS DETAILED BY THE LEFT DIVISION.
  June-Aug. 1814. 1 vol. (No. 513/415).   51
  Arranged chronologically.

          b. Miscellaneous Records, 1812-15

ORDERLY BOOK OF A RIFLE DETACHMENT COMPOSED OF SEVERAL COMPANIES FROM
  SEVERAL RIFLE REGIMENTS. Nov. 1813-May 1815. 1 vol. (No. 439/336).
  2 in.   52
  Arranged chronologically. The detachment was commanded by Col.
Thomas A. Smith, 1st Rifle Regiment, and later by Maj. Joseph Seldon,
3d Rifle Regiment; and it was a part of the Northern Army, 9th Military District. Also contains orderly book (1) of an infantry brigade
that was composed of companies of the 17th, 19th, and 24th Regiments,
and (2) of a detachment of riflemen and infantry under Col. Thomas A.
Smith, Northwestern Army, Aug.-Nov. 1813, arranged chronologically.

MISCELLANEOUS RETURNS OF THE RIGHT AND LEFT DIVISIONS. 1813-15.
  1 vol. (No. 45/507). 3 in.   53
  Arranged generally as follows: Headquarters Right Division, Headquarters Left Division, Left Division brigades, Right Division brigades, and regiments. Contains monthly, consolidated, and semiannual
returns, and registers of officers.

REGISTERS OF MEN DISCHARGED AT FORT ERIE, CHAMPLAIN STATION, GREEN-
  BUSH, PLATTSBURG, AND SACKETT'S HARBOR. 1814-15. 5 vols.
  (Nos. 556/-; 555/-; 550/-;562/-; 561/-). 6 in.   54
  Arranged by station and thereunder chronologically. Volume 556
also contains a list of British deserters and British prisoners taken
at Fort Erie, Aug.-Sept. 1814.

LISTS OF SOLDIERS WHO DIED AT VARIOUS GENERAL HOSPITALS. 1813-16.
    1 vol. (No. 566/-). 1/2 in.
    Arranged by hospital and thereunder chronologically.

REGISTERS OF PATIENTS IN THE HOSPITAL AT WILLIAMSVILLE. 1814-15.
    3 vols. (Nos. 552/-; 680/-; 683/-). 4 in.
    Arranged by time period and thereunder by regiment.

LISTS OF BRITISH PRISONERS AFTER TAKING FORT GEORGE. May 1813.
    1 vol.(n.n.).1/2 in.
    Arranged by type of list: (1) Paroled (2) placed in confinement,
(3) irregulars and (4) regulars.

LISTS OF OFFICERS AND MEN RECEIVED FROM THE BRITISH IN AN EXCHANGE OF
    MEN. 1814. 1 vol. (No. 26/397). 1 in.
    Arranged chronologically by release date. Also contains a register
of British deserters examined, 1813-14, arranged chronologically.

MISCELLANEOUS REGISTERS OF OFFICERS. 1813-14. 2 vols. (Nos. 125/320;
    126/321). 2 in.
    Arranged by type of register. Contains registers of officers on
furlough, on recruiting duty, arrested, tried, imprisoned, dismissed,
deceased, resig d, promoted, and appointed. Name index in volume 125.
Registers in volume 125 are repeated in volume 126.

REGISTER OF OFFICERS LEAVING AND REPORTING. Apr. 1814-May 1815.
    1 vol. (No. 424/311). 1 in.
    Arranged chronologically.

8. 10th Military District, 1814

     This Military District was not established until July 1814. It
was commanded by Brig. Gen. William H. Winder. About January 1815 it
was combined with the 4th Military District under Brig. Gen. Winfield
Scott.

DETAIL ORDERS. Oct.-Nov. 1814. 1 vol. (No. 511/413). 1/4 in.
    Arranged chronologically.

C. Records Relating Mainly to the 1815-21 Period

1. Division of the North

     It was composed of Military Departments Nos. 1 through 5, with head-
quarters at Brownville, N.Y., under Maj. Gen. Jacob Brown.

a. Headquarters Records, 1815-21

LETTERS SENT. Oct. 1818-May 1821. 1 vol. (No. 409/293). 2 in.   62
   Arranged chronologically. Also contains a register of letters
received and a list of resignations.

ORDERLY BOOKS. May 1815-May 1821. 2 vols. (Nos. 491/392; 518/444).
   5 in.   63
   Arranged by time period, thereunder by "received" and "sent," and
thereunder chronologically. List of contents in first volume. Contains General Orders and circulars received, and Division and special
orders issued.

REGISTER OF OFFICERS IN THE NORTHERN DIVISION. 1815. 1 vol.
   (No. 427/318). 1 in.   64
   Some names are under the Division only, and the rest are under
their departments.

REPORTS SENT TO THE SECRETARY OF WAR RELATING TO CASES OF MILITIA
   DELINQUENTS. 1818-19. 1 vol. (No. 92/317). 1/2 in.   65
   Arranged chronologically.

b. 1st and 3d Military Departments, 1818-21

   The 1st Department consisted of the States of New York, above the
Highlands, and Vermont; and the 3d consisted of the States of New York,
below the Highlands, and New Jersey, except that part which furnished
the First Division of Militia. Both were in the Division of the North,
under Maj. Gen. Jacob Brown, who in May 1815 in addition commanded
the 1st Military Department, and Bvt. Maj. Gen. Alexander Macomb the 3d
Military Department, at New York. In Sept. 1815 Brig. Gen. Moses Porter
took over the 3d Military Department, and when he was transferred to
the 2d Military Department in June 1816, he was replaced by Bvt. Maj. Gen.
Winfield Scott. At the same time Col. Hugh Brady took command of the
1st Military Department. Later both departments were commanded by Bvt.
Maj. Gen. Winfield Scott with headquarters at New York. They were
merged into the Eastern Department in 1821.

   For a volume of letters sent, see Eastern Division and Department
Progression in an inventory to be issued later.

ORDERLY BOOK. Oct. 1818-May 1821. 1 vol. (No. 470/369). 2 in.   66
   Arranged chronologically. Contains General Orders and Division
orders received, and department and special orders issued. About Dec.
1819, this volume became the record also of the 4th Military Department.

c. 5th Military Department, 1815-21

It consisted of the State of Ohio and the Territories of Michigan and Indiana, and was attached to the Division of the North, with headquarters at Detroit, Mich., under Brig. Gen. Alexander Macomb. In 1821 it was merged into the Eastern and Western Departments.

LETTERS SENT. June 1817-Jan. 1821. 1 vol. (No. 408/292). 1/2 in. <u>67</u>
   Arranged chronologically. Name index.

ORDERLY BOOK. Apr. 1818-Dec. 1820. 1 vol. (No. 468/367). 1 in. <u>68</u>
   Arranged chronologically. Contains War Department General Orders and Division orders received and department orders issued.

ORDERLY BOOK. Apr. 1818-Jan.1821. 1 vol. (No. 463/362). 2 in. <u>69</u>
   Arranged chronologically. (Partly copied, apparently from volume 468/367).

ORDERLY BOOKS OF THE BRIGADE INSPECTOR'S OFFICE. July 1815-Feb. 1818. 4 vols. (Nos. 492/393; 494/395; 441/338; 443/340). 7 in. <u>70</u>
   Arranged chronologically. Subject index in volume 443. Contains Division, department, adjutant's, and inspector's orders issued. Volume 492 also contains brigade inspector's orders announcing details, Sept.-Dec. 1815.

REGISTERS OF MEN DISCHARGED. Aug. 1815-Feb. 1821. 2 vols. (Nos. 558/-; 560/-). 2 in. <u>71</u>
   Arranged in two chronological subseries. Volume 558 was recopied in volume 560.

2. Division of the South

It was composed of Military Departments Nos. 6 through 10, with headquarters at Nashville, Tenn., under Maj. Gen. Andrew Jackson.

The records predating May 1815 are those of the 7th Military District.

a. Headquarters Records, 1813-21

LETTERS SENT. Aug. 1814-July 1815; Apr. 1816-Jan. 1821. 2 vols. (n.n.; No. 407/291). 3 in. <u>72</u>
   Arranged chronologically. Name index in second volume.

ORDERLY BOOKS OF THE ADJUTANT GENERAL. June 1813-Feb. 1821. 3 vols. (Nos. 391/275; 454/353; 65/212). 6 in. <u>73</u>
   Arranged chronologically except that volume 454 follows after page 123 in volume 391.

ORDERLY BOOK OF THE ADJUTANT GENERAL. June 1813-Nov. 1814. 1 vol.
   (No. 433/330). 1 in.   <u>74</u>
   Arranged generally chronologically. Orders for the period June-Nov.
1814 have been recopied in volume 454; and those for the period June
1813-June 1814, in volume 391 (see entry 73).

b. <u>8th Military Department, 1815-21</u>

      The Department consisted of the State of Louisiana and the
Territory of Mississippi, and attached to the Division of the South,
under Brig. Gen. Elez W. Ripley and Brig. Gen. Daniel Bissell,with
headquarters at New Orleans. In 1821, it was merged into the Western
Department.

      For an additional orderly book beginning February 1820, see
Western Division and Department Progression in an inventory to be
issued later.

LETTERS SENT. May 1817-May 1821. 1 vol. 1 in.   <u>75</u>
   Arranged chronologically.

ORDERLY BOOKS OF THE ADJUTANT GENERAL. Sept. 1815-Oct. 1816; Dec.
   1816-Jan. 18 . 3 vols. (n.n.; n.n.; No.435/332). 2 in.   <u>76</u>
   Arranged chronologically.

ORDERLY BOOK OF THE BRIGADE MAJOR AT NEW ORLEANS. Apr. 1815-Mar. 1816.
   1 vol. (No. 484/385). 1/2 in.   <u>77</u>
   Arranged chronologically. The brigade major was with the Western
Section, 7th Military District, and the 8th Military Department.

c. <u>9th Military Department</u>

      The Department consisted of the States of Tennessee and Kentucky
and the Territories of Missouri and Illinois, and was attached to the
Division of the South, with headquarters at Bellefontaine and St. Louis,
in the Territory of Missouri, under Bvt. Brig. Gen. Thomas A. Smith
and Brig. Gen. Henry Atkinson. It was merged into the Eastern and Western Departments in 1821.

      For an orderly book beginning June 1819, see Western Division and
Department Progression in an inventory to be issued later.

3. <u>Records of Bvt. Maj. Gen. Edmund P. Gaines, 1814-19</u>

LETTERS SENT AND RECEIVED BY GENERAL GAINES. 1814; 1817-19. 2 vols.
   (n.n.; n.n.). 3 in.   <u>78</u>
   Arranged chronologically, with gaps. Name index in first volume.

First volume c[ ]ers the following: Jan.-May 1814 at Sackett's Harbor, 9th Military District; Sept.-Dec. 1814, 4th Military District; and Mar. 1815, 7th Military District. The second volume covers: Eastern Section, Division of the South; 7th Military Department, and Post of Fernandina, East Florida.

III. Records of Units

    A. Artillery

        1. Regiment of Light Artillery, 1808-21

           This regiment existed from 1808 to 1821.

        a. Orderly Books

ORDERLY BOOK OF THE REGIMENT. Mar.-June 1814. 1 vol. (n.n.).
  1 in.   79
  Arranged chronologically. Contains 9th Military District, Northern Army, and War Department General Orders received, and regimental orders issued.

ORDERLY BOOKS OF COMPANY H. June 1815-Jan. 1818. 3 vols. (Nos.
  493/394; 448/346; 444/341). 3 in.   80
  Arranged generally chronologically except that orders for the period Apr.-June 1817, which follows those in volume 448, are found at the back of volume 493. Contain Northern Division, 2d Military Department, garrison, detachment, and regimental orders received, and company orders issued.

ORDERLY BOOKS OF THE BATTALION AT FORT INDEPENDENCE. May 1818-Mar.
  1819; Sept. 1819-Oct. 1820. 2 vols. (Nos. 462/361; 517/443).
  2 in.   81
  Arranged by time period and thereunder by orders received and orders issued. Contain War Department General Orders, 2d Military Department Orders, and Northern Division Orders received; and regimental and detachment orders issued.

        b. Company Books

COMPANY BOOKS FOR THE COMPANY OF CAPT. HENRY K. CRAIG. 1815-21.
  2 vols. (Nos. 173/6; 174/8A). 5 in.   82
  Arranged by time period and thereunder by type of record. List of contents in volume 173/6.

COMPANY BOOKS FOR THE COMPANY OF CAPT. WILLIAM F. HOBART. 1817-21.
    2 vols. (Nos. 171/5; 172/7). 4 in.   83
    Arranged by type of record.

COMPANY BOOK FOR THE COMPANY OF CAPT. WILLIAM N. IRVINE. 1808-9
    1 vol. (No. 365/8B). 1 in.   84
    Arranged by type of record. Name index.

COMPANY BOOK FOR THE COMPANY OF CAPT. LUTHER LEONARD. 1812-15.
    1 vol. (No. 169/3). 1 in.   85
    Arranged by type of record.

COMPANY BOOK FOR THE COMPANY OF LT. GEORGE N. MORRIS AND CAPT. JOHN
    R. BELL. 1814-15. 1 vol. (No. 170/4). 1 in.   86
    Arranged by type of record.

c. Other Records

MORNING REPORTS. Oct. 1814-Feb. 1815. 1 vol. (No. 363/205A).
    1 in.   87
    Arranged chronologically.

MORNING REPORTS FOR THE BATTALION FORMING THE GARRISON AT FORT INDE-
    PENDENCE, BOSTON HARBOR. June 1817-Oct. 1818; Feb. 1819-Mar. 1820.
    3 vols. (Nos. 352/208; 353/209; 354/210). 8 in.   88
    Arranged chronologically. After Feb. 1819 these reports frequently
include those for light artillery companies stationed at forts in the
vicinity of Fort Independence.

MORNING REPORTS FOR THE BATTALION AT GREENBUSH AND PLATTSBURG, N.Y.
    Feb. 1815-Dec. 1816. 2 vols. (Nos. 350/205B; 351/207). 4 in.   89
    Arranged chronologically. Volume 351 also contains morning reports
for the battalion forming the garrison at Fort Independence, Oct. 1818-
Feb. 1819, that fit between the reports in volumes 353 and 354 of
series 88.

MONTHLY RETURNS. 1816-19. 1 vol. (No. 36/232). 2 in.   90
    Arranged chronologically.

RECEIPTS FOR CLOTHING FOR THE COMPANY OF CAPT. HENRY K. CRAIG.
    1817-19. 1 vol. (No. 98/-). 1/2 in.   91
    Arranged chronologically.

INSPECTION RETURNS OF THE REGIMENT OF LIGHT ARTILLERY. 1819-21.
    1 vol. (No. 39/296). 4 in.   92
    Arranged chronologically.

MISCELLANEOUS RECORDS. 1811-21. 1 vol. (No. 41/206). 1 in.   <u>93</u>
    Arranged by type of record as follows: Descriptive rolls; morning
reports; monthly returns; and registers of promotions, transfers, and
desertions.

2. Nu _ered Regiments

    All records of the following regiments extending beyond May 1814
became records of the Corps of Artillery.

a. 1st(1802-14) Regiment, 1803-15

ORDERLY BOOK FOR THE COMPANY OF CAPT. AMOS STODDARD. Nov. 1807-June
    1808. 1 vol. (No. 482/383). 1 in.   <u>94</u>
    Arranged chronologically. Captain Stoddard was commanding the
garrison at Fort Adams, Miss., from Nov. 1807 to June 1808 and Fort
Dearborn, Miss., from June to Sept. 1808.

ORDERLY BOOK FOR THE COMPANY OF CAPT. WILLIAM L. COOPER. Dec. 1803-
    July 1804. 1 vol. (No. 367/233). 1 in.   <u>95</u>
    Arranged chronologically. Captain Cooper's Company was the company
composing the garrison at Plaquemine, La., and Balize, La., from Dec.
1803 to May 1804, and part of the garrison at New Orleans from May to
July 1804. Also contains similar records for an unidentified company
accompanying Gen. James Wilkinson from Fort Adams to New Orleans during Nov. and Dec. 1803. This may also be Cooper's Company.

COMPANY BOOK FOR THE COMPANY OF CAPT. THOMAS BENNETT. 1810-15. 1 vol.
    (No. 184/18). 1 in.   <u>96</u>
    Arranged by type of record. Name index.

COMPANY BOOK FOR THE COMPANY OF CAPT. JULIUS F. HEILEMAN. 1813-15.
    1 vol. (No. 194/26). 2 in.   <u>97</u>
    Arranged by type of record. Name index.

COMPANY BOOK FOR THE COMPANY OF CAPT. JAMES HOUSE. 1806-11. 1 vol.
    (No. 177/11). 1 in.   <u>98</u>
    Arranged by type of record. Name index.

COMPANY BOOK FOR THE COMPANY OF CAPT. JAMES REED. 1812-15. 1 vol.
    (No. 187/21). 1 in.   <u>99</u>
    Arranged by type of record.

MONTHLY RETURNS OF THE ARTILLERY TROOPS AT NEW ORLEANS AND FORT ST.
    PHILLIP, LA. 1807-11. 1 vol. (No. 528/235). 1 in.   <u>100</u>
    Arranged chronologically. Also contains a register of discharges.

b. 2d (1812-14) Regiment, 1812-15

COMPANY BOOKS FOR THE COMPANY OF CAPT. JAMES N. BARKER. 1812-15.
  2 vols. (Nos. 178/12B; 189/12A). 2 in.   <u>101</u>
    Arranged by time period and thereunder by type of record. List
of contents in volume 189.

COMPANY BOOK FOR THE COMPANY OF CAPTS. JOHN RITCHIE AND ALEXANDER C.
  W. FANNING. 1812-14. 1 vol. (No. 186/20). 1 in.   <u>102</u>
    Arranged by type of record. Captain Fanning took command in August
1814, after the 2d regiment had become a part of the Corps of Artillery.

COMPANY BOOK FOR THE COMPANY OF CAPT. MOSES SWETT. 1812-15. 1 vol.
  (No. 183/17). 2 in.   <u>103</u>
    Arranged by type of record. Name index.

COMPANY BOOK FOP THE COMPANY OF CAPT. ALEXANDER J. WILLIAMS. 1813-15.
  1 vol. (No. 32/16). 1 in.   <u>104</u>
    Arranged by type of record.

CLOTHING BOOK FOR THE COMPANY OF CAPTS. JOHN RITCHIE AND ALEXANDER C.
  W. FANNING. 1812-15. 1 vol. (No. 175/9). 1 in.   <u>105</u>
    Arranged by name of individual. Partial name index. Captain
Fanning took command in August 1814, after the 2d regiment had become
a part of the Corps of Artillery.

c. 3d (1812-14) Regiment, 1812-15

ORDERLY BOOK. Dec. 1813. 1 vol. (No. 397/280). 1 in.   <u>106</u>
    Arranged chronologically.

COMPANY BOOK FOR THE COMPANY OF CAPT. ICHABOD B. CRANE. 1812-15.
  1 vol. (No. 197/29). 1 in.   <u>107</u>
    Arranged by type of record.

COMPANY BOOK FOR THE COMPANY OF CAPT. ALEXANDER C. W. FANNING.
  1812-15. 1 vol. (No. 190/23A). 1 in.   <u>108</u>
    Arranged by type of record.

COMPANY BOOK FOR THE COMPANY OF CAPT. RUFUS McINTIRE. 1812-15.
  1 vol. (No. 192/24). 1 in.   <u>109</u>
    Arranged by type of record.

COMPANY BOOK FOR THE COMPANY OF CAPT. BENJAMIN K. PIERCE. 1813-15.
  1 vol. (No. 188/22). 1 in.   <u>110</u>
    Arranged by type of record.

COMPANY BOOK FOR THE COMPANY OF CAPT. JAMES T. B. ROMAYNE. 1812-16.
    1 vol. (No. 179/13). 1 in.   111
    Arranged by type of record. Name index.

COMPANY BOOK FOR THE COMPANY OF CAPT. HORACE H. WATSON. 1812-17.
    1 vol. (No. 176/10). 2 in.   112
    Arranged by type of record. Name index.

COMPANY BOOK FOR THE COMPANY OF CAPT. WILLIAM VAN DEURSEN, JR. 1812-14.
    1 vol. (No. 181/15). 1 in.   113
    Arranged by type of record. Name index.

CLOTHING BOOK FOR THE COMPANY OF CAPTS. ALEXANDER C. W. FANNING AND
    ROGER JONES. 1812-15. 1 vol. (No. 191/23B). 1 in.   114
    Arranged by type of record. List of contents.

3. Corps of Artillery, 1814-21

    This Corps existed from 1814 to 1821.

ORDERLY BOOK OF THE 4TH BATTALION. 1818-22. 1 vol. (n.n.). 1 in. 115
    Arranged chronologically. Contains War Department General Orders,
Division orders, 8th Military Department orders, and some letters
received.

COMPANY BOOK FOR THE COMPANY OF CAPT. THOMAS BIDDLE. 1818-21.
    1 vol. (No. 238/94). 1 in.   116
    Arranged by type of record. Name index.

COMPANY BOOK FOR THE COMPANY OF CAPT. JAMES H. BOYLES. 1814-15.
    1 vol. (No. 195/27). 1 in.   117
    Arranged by type of record.

COMPANY BOOK FOR THE COMPANY OF CAPTS. LOWNDES BROWN AND GREENLEAF
    DEARBORN. 1818-21. 1 vol. (No. 198/30). 4 in.   118
    Arranged by type of record. Name index.

COMPANY BOOK FOR THE COMPANY OF CAPT. JAMES R. HANHAM. 1814-15.
    1 vol. (No. 180/14). 2 in.   119
    Arranged by type of record.

COMPANY BOOK FOR THE COMPANY OF CAPT. JULIUS HEILEMAN. 1818-22.
    1 vol. (n.n.). 3 in.   120
    Arranged by type of record.

ORDERLY AND COMPANY BOOK FOR THE COMPANY OF CAPT. BENJAMIN K. PIERCE.
     1815-18. 1 vol.(No. 688/-). 1 in.   121
     Arranged by orders and company book information; orders arranged
thereunder chronologically, and company book information arranged thereunder by type of record. The orders are War Department, Division of the
North, and 5th Military Department General Orders.

COMPANY BOOK FOR THE COMPANY OF CAPT. RICHARD A. ZANTZINGER AND LT.
     ROBERT STEWART. 1814-15. 1 vol. (No. 196/28). 1 in.   122
     Arranged by type of record.

          B. Dragoons: Regiment of Light Dragoons, 1812-15

     This regiment existed from 1808 to 1815.

COMPANY BOOKS FOR THE COMPANY OF CAPT. JOHN A. BURD. 1812-15.
     2 vols. (Nos. 167/2A; 168/2B). 2 in.   123
     Arranged by time period and thereunder by type of record.

COMPANY BOOK FOR THE COMPANY OF CAPT. WILLIAM LITTLEJOHN. 1813-15.
     1 vol. (No. 166/1). 1 in.   124
     Arranged by type of record.

          C. Infantry

               1. Records Relating to the 1784-89 Period

                    a. First (1784) American Regiment, 1784

INSPECTION RETURN OF THE AMERICAN REGIMENT OF FOOT UNDER COL. HENRY
     JACKSON. May 1784. 1 vol. 1/4 in.   125

                    b. 1st (1784-89) Regiment, 1785-88

LETTERS SENT AND RECEIVED BY CAPT. JONATHAN HEART, COMPANY COMMANDER.
     Apr. 1787-Jan. 1788. 1 vol. 1/2 in.   126
     Arranged chronologically. These are chiefly letters sent to and
received from Lt. Col.Josiah Harmar, commanding the 1st Regiment.

ORDERLY BOOK FOR COMPANY OF CAPT. JONATHAN HEART. Sept. 1785-May 1788.
     1 vol. 1/2 in.   127
     Arranged chronologically.

               2. Records Relating to the 1789-1815 Period

     The reader will notice that many volumes extend beyond May 1815,
the date of the reorganization of the infantry, and beyond June 1815,

the discharge date for many of the officers. It appears from the
records that it was sometimes as late as Aug. 1815 that notices of
reorganization and of discharges were received.

a. 1st (1789-1815) Regiment, 1807-15

For the years 1792-96, this regiment was designated the 1st Sub-
legion.

COMPANY BOOK FOR THE COMPANY OF CAPTS. JOHN SYMMES AND ELI B. CLEMSON.
   1807-15. 1 vol. (No. 53/41). 3 in.   128
   Arranged by type of record. Name index.

COMPANY BOOK FOR THE COMPANY OF CAPT. SIMON OWENS. 1810-14. 1 vol.
   (No. 52/40). 2 in.   129
   Arranged by type of record. Name index.

COMPANY BOOK FOR THE COMPANY OF CAPT. HORATIO STARK. 1812-15.
   1 vol. (No. 223/83A). 1 in.   130
   Arranged by type of record. Name index.

COMPANY BOOK FOR THE COMPANY OF CAPTS. LAURENCE TALIAFERRO AND
   LINAI T. HELM, 1813-14. 1 vol. (No. 54/42). 1 in.   131
   Arranged by type of record. Name index.

COMPANY BOOK FOR THE COMPANY OF CAPT. JOHN WHISTLER. 1811-12.
   1 vol. (No. 226/85). 1/2 in.   132
   Arranged by type of record. Name index.

COMPANY BOOK FOR THE COMPANY OF CAPTS. JOHN WHISTLER AND JAMES RHEA.
   1812-15. 1 vol. (No. 55/43). 1 in.   133
   Arranged by type of record. Also contains a descriptive list en-
titled "Hugh Moore's 1st Infantry."

b. 2d (1791-1815) Regiment, 1802-15

For the years 1792-96, this regiment was designated the 2d Sub-
legion. Unless otherwise stated, the companies of the 2d regiment whose
orderly books are described below were at the following stations:

May 1808-Nov. 1810	Columbian Springs and Contonment, 2d Regiment, near Washington, Mississippi Territory
Dec. 1810-Mar. 1811	Baton Rouge, La.
Mar. 1811-May 1812	Fort Stoddert, Ala.
May 1812-Feb. 1813	Mt. Vernon, near Fort Stoddert, Ala.
Mar. 1813-Dec. 1813	In and around New Orleans, La.; and Camp Perdido, Mobile, and Fort Charlotte, Ala.

```
Jan. 1814-Mar. 1815    Fort Bowyer, Ala. (Fort Morgan)
Mar. 1815-May  1815    New Orleans, La.
May  1815-Sept.1815    Pass Christian, Miss.
```

(1) Orderly Books

From 1813 to 1815 the 2d Regiment was in the 7th Military Districts Therefore, the orderly books will normally contain War Department and 7th Military District General Orders, as well as garrison and regimental orders.

ORDERLY BOOK PROBABLY OF CAPT. MATTHEW ARBUCKLE'S COMPANY AT CAMP
    NATCHITOCHES. Nov. 1804-July 1805. 1 vol. (No. 431/328). 1 in.   134
    Contains War Department and Gen. James Wilkinson's General Orders,
New Orleans garrison orders, and detachment orders.

ORDERLY BOOK FOR THE COMPANY OF CAPT. MATTHEW ARBUCKLE. May 1812-Jan.
    1813. 1 vol. (No. 120/245). 1 in.   135
    Arranged chronologically.

ORDERLY BOOK FOR THE COMPANY OF CAPT. WILLIAM R. BOOTE. 1810-12.
    1 vol. (No. 118/242). 1 in.   136
    Arranged chronologically. Captain Boote commanded the post of Fort
Hawkins, Ga., in the Southern Department.

ORDERLY BOOK OF A DETACHMENT OR COMPANY OF CAPT. JOSEPH BOWMAR AT
    NATCHITOCHES, LA. Mar.-Sept. 1806. 1 vol. (No. 504/406). 1 in.   137
    Arranged chronologically. Contains district and regimental orders.
Also contains orderly book of a company at Fort Adams and Camp Columbian Springs, 2d Regiment, June-Sept. 1807, which is arranged chronologically.

ORDERLY BOOKS FOR THE COMPANY OF CAPT. WILLIAM LAWRENCE. Dec.
    1809-Dec. 1813; Dec. 1814-Aug. 1815. 5 vols. (Nos. 475/376; 485/
    386; 123/247; 471/370; 122/248). 5 in.   138
    Arranged chronologically. Volume 123 also contains an orderly book
for an unidentified company, 2d Regiment, at Mobile Point and Fort
Charlotte, July-Dec. 1813, which is arranged chronologically.

ORDERLY BOOK OF AN UNIDENTIFIED COMPANY STATIONED AT NEW ORLEANS.
    Apr. 1805-July 1806. 1 vol. (No. 113/237). 1 in.   139
    Arranged chronologically. Lt. Josiah Taylor was adjutant of this
company. Contains only district and garrison orders issued by Lt. Col.
Constant Freeman.

ORDERLY BOOKS OF AN UNIDENTIFIED COMPANY. May 1808-Aug. 1810.
   3 vols. (Nos. 114/238; 115/239; 116/240). 2 in.   <u>140</u>
   Arranged chronologically.

ORDERLY BOOKS OF AN UNIDENTIFIED COMPANY. Aug. 1809-May 1811.
   2 vols. (Nos. 117/241; 119/243). 2 in.   <u>141</u>
   Arranged chronologically.

ORDERLY BOOK OF AN UNIDENTIFIED COMPANY. Dec. 1810-Feb. 1811.
   1 vol. (No. 130/374). 1/2 in.   <u>142</u>
   Arranged chronologically. Also contains rosters of Capt. William
Lawrence's Company, Nov. 1812-Feb. 1813.

ORDERLY BOOK FOR AN UNIDENTIFIED COMPANY. Sept. 1813-June 1814.
   1 vol. (No. 490/391). 1/2 in.   <u>143</u>
   Arranged chronologically.

(2) <u>Company Books</u>

COMPANY BOOK FOR THE COMPANY OF CAPT. WILLIAM R. BOOTE. 1805-10.
   1 vol. (No. 110/59A). 1 in.   <u>144</u>
   Arranged by type of record. All men in this company were transferred or discharged before another company commanded by Captain Boote
(see entry 145) was formed.

COMPANY BOOK FOR THE COMPANY OF CAPT. WILLIAM R. BOOTE. 1812-14.
   1 vol. (No. 111/59B). 1 in.   <u>145</u>
   Arranged by type of record. List of contents.

COMPANY BOOK FOR THE COMPANY OF CAPTS. WILLIAM BOOTE AND WILLIAM
   LAWRENCE. 1812-14. 1 vol. (No. 42/244). 1/2 in.   <u>146</u>
   Arranged by type of record. List of contents.

COMPANY BOOK FOR THE COMPANY OF CAPTS. JOHN BRAHAN AND REUBEN CHAMBER-
   LAIN. 1807-9. 1 vol. (No. 106/55). 1/2 in.   <u>147</u>
   Arranged by type of record. Name index.

COMPANY BOOK FOR THE COMPANY OF CAPTS. JOHN BRAHAN AND WILLIAM
   LAWRENCE. 1807-13. 1 vol. (No. 108/57). 1 in.   <u>148</u>
   Arranged by type of record. Name index.

COMPANY BOOK FOR THE COMPANY OF CAPTS. JOHN CAMPBELL AND ROBERT PURDY.
   1803-7. 1 vol. (No. 104/53). 1 in.   <u>149</u>
   Arranged by type of record. Name index.

COMPANY BOOK FOR THE COMPANY OF CAPTS. JOHN CAMPBELL AND JOHN R.
    LUCKETT. 1807-13. 1 vol. (No. 105/54). 1 in.   150
    Arranged by type of record. Name index.

COMPANY BOOK FOR THE COMPANY OF CAPT. REUBEN CHAMBERLAIN. 1813-15.
    1 vol. (No. 107/56). 1 in.   151
    Arranged by type of record. Name index. Also contains hospital
sick returns at Fort St. Phillip, Sept.-Oct. 1816.

COMPANY BOOK FOR THE COMPANY OF CAPTS. WILLIAM LAWRENCE, HEZEKIAH
    BRADLEY, AND ALEXANDER GRAY. 1812-16. 1 vol. (No. 109/58).
    1 in.   152
    Arranged by type of record. Name index. After May 1815 this vol-
ume was the company book of Captain Gray, 1st Infantry Regiment.

COMPANY BOOK FOR THE COMPANY OF CAPT. RICHARD SPARKS. 1802-5. 1 vol.
    (No. 112/60). 1 in.   153
    Arranged by type of record.

(3) Other Records

REGISTERS OF DISCHARGES, DEATHS, AND DESERTIONS; LIST OF OFFICERS;
    AND DESCRIPTIVE ROLLS OF COMPANIES. 1811-14. 1 vol. (No. 103/52).
    2 in.   154
    Arranged by type of record. List of contents.

MORNING REPORTS AND ROSTERS FOR THE COMPANY OF CAPT. WILLIAM LAWRENCE.
    Mar.-Oct. 1812. 1 vol. (No. 121/246). 1/2 in.   155
    Arranged chronologically. Rosters are continued in volume 130,
series 142.

c. 3d (1796-1802) Regiment, 1796-1802

ORDERLY BOOK FOR THE COMPANY OF CAPT. JOHN STEELE. May-Oct. 1799.
    1 vol. (No. 480/381). 1/2 in.   156
    Arranged chronologically. Steele's Company was located at Camp
Loftus' Heights, Mississippi Territory. Also contains rosters of
noncommissioned officers and abstracts of morning reports.

ORDERLY BOOKS OF THE ADJUTANT AT FORT ADAMS. Feb. 1801-June 1802.
    2 vols. (Nos. 162/249; 129/371). 2 in.   157
    Arranged chronologically. Also contains orderly books of Capt.
Richard Sparks, 2d Regiment, ca. June 1802-Jan. 1804, at Fort Adams,
arranged chronologically. Orders received were War Department and
Gen. James Wilkinson's General Orders, and district and garrison
orders.

COMPANY BOOK FOR THE COMPANY OF CAPT. RICHARD SPARKS. 1796-1800.
   1 vol. (No. 153/61). 1/2 in.   158
   Arranged by type of record.

         d.   3d (1808-15) Regiment, 1808-15 —

   Unless otherwise stated, the companies of the 3d regiment whose orderly books are described below were at the following stations:

Feb. 1812-Aug. 1812	Cantonment St. Tammany and Baton Rouge, La.
Aug. 1812-Nov. 1812	Pass Christian, Miss.
Dec. 1812-June 1813	New Orleans, La., and Cantonment English Turn.
June 1813-July 1813	Cantonment opposite New Orleans, La.
Aug. 1813-Sept.1813	In and around Cantonment Washington, Miss.
Oct. 1813-Nov. 1813	Mt. Vernon, near Fort Stoddert, Ala.
Dec. 1813-June 1814	Fort Claiborne and Alabama Heights, Ala.
July 1814-Aug. 1814	Fort Jackson, Ala.
Aug. 1814-Dec. 1814	Camp 3d Regiment.
Dec. 1814-Feb. 1815	Camp Lance Mandeville and Camp Bayou, La.
Mar. 1815-May 1815	New Orleans, La.
May 1815-Aug. 1815	Pass Christian, Miss.

   From 1813 to 1815 the 3d regiment was in the 7th Military District. Therefore the orderly books will normally contain War Department and 7th Military District General Orders, as well as garrison and regimental orders.

         (1) Orderly Books

ORDERLY BOOK FOR THE COMPANY OF CAPT. SAMUEL W. BUTLER. Jan.-Apr.
   1815. 1 vol. (No. 165/252). 1 in.   159
   Arranged chronologically.

ORDERLY BOOKS FOR THE COMPANY OF CAPT. JOSEPH DINKINS. Feb. 1812-
   July 1814. 2 vols. (Nos. 498/400; 474/375). 2 in.   160
   Arranged by time period, and thereunder in two subseries: (1)
those received from the 3d Regiment and (2) others received.

ORDERLY BOOK FOR THE COMPANY OF CAPT. THOMAS HUNTER. Apr.-Dec. 1815.
   1 vol. (No. 497/399). 1 in.   161
   Arranged chronologically. From Sept. to Dec. 1815 this is the
orderly book of an unidentified company of the 1st Infantry.

ORDERLY BOOKS FOR THE COMPANY OF CAPTS. JOSEPH WOODRUFF AND SAMUEL MAB-
   SON. Oct. 1813-Dec. 1814. 2 vols. (Nos. 163/250; 164/251). 2 in.162
   Arranged chronologically.

ORDERLY BOOK FOR AN UNIDENTIFIED COMPANY. May-Aug. 1815. 1 vol.
   (No. 473/373). 1/2 in.   163
   Arranged chronologically.

ORDERLY BOOKS FOR AN UNIDENTIFIED COMPANY. Nov. 1814-Feb. 1815.
2 vols. (Nos. 438/335; 496/398). 1 in.
Arranged chronologically.

(2) Company Books

COMPANY BOOKS FOR THE COMPANY OF CAPT. WILLIAM BUTLER. 1810-14.
2 vols. (Nos. 155/63; 156/64). 2 in.
Arranged by time period and thereunder by type of record.

COMPANY BOOK FOR THE COMPANY OF CAPTS. SAMUEL W. BUTLER, WILLIAM
LAVAL, AND JOHN McCLELLAND. 1812-15. 1 vol. (No. 157/65).
1 in.
Arranged by type of record.

COMPANY BOOK FOR THE COMPANY OF CAPT. JAMES E. DINKINS. 1812-15.
1 vol. (No. 160/68). 1 in.
Arranged by type of record. List of contents.

COMPANY BOOK FOR THE COMPANY OF CAPT. SAMUEL C. MABSON. 1812-15.
1 vol. (No. 159/67). 1 in.
Arranged by type of record. Name index.

COMPANY BOOK FOR THE COMPANY OF CAPTS. ROBERT B. MOORE AND HENRY
CHOTARD. 1812-15. 1 vol. (No. 158/66). 1/2 in.
Arranged by type of record.

COMPANY BOOK FOR THE COMPANY OF CAPT. JOSEPH WOODRUFF. 1809-15.
1 vol. (No. 154/62). 1 in.
Arranged by type of record.

(3) Other Records

MUSTER ROLLS. 1808-13. 1 vol. 3 in.
Arranged by company (Capt. Henry Atkinson's, Capt. Samuel Butler's,
Capt. Ross Bird's, Capt. William Butler's, Lt. Wm. Davis', and Capt.
James E. Dinkin's companies).

4th (1808-15) Regiment, 1811-12

LETTERS SENT AND RECEIVED AND ORDERS ISSUED AND RECEIVED. Apr. 1811-
May 1812. 1 vol. (No. 685/-). 2 in.
Arranged chronologically. Also contains quarterly, half yearly,
officers' and monthly returns, 1st Battalion, 41st Infantry, May-Oct.
1813, which are arranged by "monthly returns" and "other returns" and
thereunder chronologically.

f. 5th (1808-15) Regiment, 1810-15

COMPANY BOOK FOR THE COMPANY OF CAPT. RICHARD H. BELL. 1810-14.
    1 vol. (No. 209/71). 1 in.   <u>173</u>
    Arranged by type of record. Name and subject index.

COMPANY BOOK FOR THE COMPANY OF CAPTS. JAMES DORMAN AND JOHN JAMISON.
    1814-15. 1 vol. (No. 208/70). 1 in.   <u>174</u>
    Arranged by type of record. Name and subject index.

MONTHLY RETURNS AND MUSTER ROLLS FOR COMPANY OF CAPT. BENJAMIN ROPE.
    1814-15. 1 vol. 1/2 in.   <u>175</u>
    Arranged chronologically. Also contains quarterly and monthly
returns for the company of Capt. James Pratt, 5th Infantry, 1815-18,
which are arranged chronologically.

g. 6th (1808-15) Regiment, 1811-15

LETTERS SENT AND RECEIVED. June 1811-Oct. 1813. 1 vol. 2 in.   <u>176</u>
    Arranged chronologically.

COMPANY BOOK FOR THE COMPANY OF CAPT. JOHN CHAPMAN. 1814-15.
    1 vol. (No. 211/73). 1 in.   <u>177</u>
    Arranged by type of record. List of contents and name index.

COMPANY BOOK FOR THE COMPANY OF CAPTS. GAD HUMPHREYS AND JAMES
    BAILEY. 1813-15. 1 vol. (No. 212/74). 1 in.   <u>178</u>
    Arranged by type of record. Name index.

COMPANY BOOK FOR THE COMPANY OF CAPT. JAMES MASTERS. 1811-15.
    1 vol. (No. 210/72). 1 in.   <u>179</u>
    Arranged by type of record.

h. 7th (1808-15) Regiment, 1808-15

    Unless otherwise stated, the companies of the 7th regiment, whose
orderly books are described below, were at the following stations:

Feb.	1812-Aug. 1812	Baton Rouge, La.
Aug.	1812-Sept.1812	New Orleans, La.
Sept.	1812-Dec. 1812	Pass Christian, Miss.
Dec.	1812-July 1813	New Orleans, La.
July	1813-Aug. 1813	Pass Christian, Miss.
Aug.	1813-Sept.1813	Mobile, Ala.
Sept.	1813-Nov. 1813	Fort Charlotte, Ala.
Nov.	1813-June 1814	New Orleans, La.

June 1814   Pass Christian, Miss.
July 1814-Oct. 1814 Tchefonte, Mississippi Ter.
Oct. 1814-Feb. 1815 New Orleans, La.
Feb. 1815   Camp Jackson, La.
Mar. 1815-June 1815 P.M. Barracks, New Orleans, La.

From 1813 to 1815 the 7th Regiment was in the 7th Military District. Therefore the orderly books will normally contain War Department and 7th Military District General Orders, as well as garrison and regimental orders.

(1) Orderly Books

ORDERLY BOOKS. Sept. 1813-June 1815. 3 vols. (Nos. 428/325; 95/-; 378/262). 3 in.
    Arranged chronologically.   180

ORDERLY BOOKS OF CAPT. RICHARD OLDHAM'S COMPANY. May-Oct. 1812; Jan.-June 1814. 2 vols. (Nos. 372/256; 100/-). 2 in.
    Arranged chronologically.   181

ORDERLY BOOKS OF CAPT. SAMUEL VAIL'S COMPANY. Oct. 1814-Sept. 1815. 2 vols. (Nos. 480/387; 96/-). 2 in.
    Arranged chronologically.   182

ORDERLY BOOK OF A DETACHMENT UNDER CAPT. WM. McCLELLAN EN ROUTE TO NEW ORLEANS FROM KNOXVILLE. June 1813-Dec. 1814. 1 vol. (No. 375/259). 1 in.   183
    Arranged chronologically. From Mar. to Dec. 1814 this is the record presumably of a company of the 7th Regiment, probably McClellan's.

ORDERLY BOOKS OF AN UNIDENTIFIED COMPANY. Feb. 1812-Jan. 1814. 3 vols. (Nos. 370/253; 374/258; 97/-). 3 in.   184
    Arranged generally chronologically. Contains one letter and a few orders of Generals Wilkinson, Hampton, and Gansevoort, 1809-10.

ORDERLY BOOKS OF AN UNIDENTIFIED COMPANY. Feb. 1812-Jan. 1814. 3 vols. (Nos. 371/255; 373/257; 376/260). 3 in.   185
    Arranged generally chronologically.

(2) Company Books

COMPANY BOOK FOR THE COMPANY OF CAPT. JAMES DOHERTY. 1808-11. 1 vol. (No. 362/423). 1 in.   186
    Arranged by type of record. All men in this company were transferred or discharged before another company commanded by Captain Doherty (see entry 187) was formed.

COMPANY BOOK FOR THE COMPANY OF CAPT. JAMES DOHERTY. 1813-15.
    1 vol. (No. 214/76). 1 in.   187
    Arranged by type of record

COMPANY BOOK FOR THE COMPANY OF CAPT. WALTER H. OVERTON. 1811-15.
    1 vol. (No. 213/75). 1 in.   188
    Arranged by type of record.

(3) Other Records

REPORTS OF STRENGTH AND DETAILS FOR GUARD DUTY AT THE GARRISON OF
    NEW ORLEANS. 1812-15. 1 vol. (No. 361/421). 1/2 in.   189
    Arranged chronologically.

ROSTERS OF NONCOMMISSIONED OFFICERS OF THE 7TH REGIMENT. 1812-14.
    1 vol. (No. 94/323). 1/2 in.   190
    Arranged chronologically and thereunder by rank.

MORNING REPORTS. 1813-15. 4 vols. (Nos. 425/312; 355/254;
    377/261; 379/263). 4 in.   191
    Arranged chronologically. Volume 355 also contains morning
reports of the detachment of the 7th Infantry at Baton Rouge,
Nov. 1811-Feb. 1812, which are arranged chronologically.

i. 9th (1812-15) Regiment, 1812-15

COMPANY BOOK FOR THE COMPANY OF CAPTS. GEORGE BENDER AND SAMUEL
    ALLEN. 1813-15. 1 vol. (No. 219/80B). 2 in.   192
    Arranged by type of record.

COMPANY BOOK FOR THE COMPANY OF LT. DANIEL CHANDLER. 1814-15.
    1 vol. (No. 224/83B). 2 in.   193
    Arranged by type of record.

COMPANY BOOK FOR THE COMPANY OF CAPT. WILLIAM L. FOSTER. 1814.
    1 vol. (No. 222/82). 1 in.   194
    Arranged by type of record.

COMPANY BOOK FOR THE COMPANY OF CAPT. ABRAHAM F. HULL. 1814.
    1 vol. (No. 221/81B). 1 in.   195
    Arranged by type of record.

COMPANY BOOK FOR THE COMPANY OF CAPTS. ABRAHAM F. HULL AND MOSES
    HOIT. 1812-15. 1 vol. (No. 220/81A). 1 in.   196
    Arranged by type of record.

DESCRIPTIVE LIST OF CAPT. CHESTER LYMAN'S COMPANY. 1812-13.
   1 vol. (No. 218/80A). 1 in.   197
     Arranged chronologically by date of enlistment. Later became
Capt. George Bender's Company.

j. 10th (1812-15) Regiment, 1813-15

COMPANY BOOK FOR THE COMPANY OF CAPT. GEORGE VASHON. 1813-15. 1 vol.
   (No. 225/84). 1 in.   198
     Arranged by type of record.

k. 11th (1812-15) Regiment, 1812-15

COMPANY BOOK FOR THE COMPANY OF CAPTS. RICHARD BEAN AND MALACHI
   CORNING. 1813-14. 1 vol. (No. 234/91). 1 in.   199
     Arranged by type of record.

COMPANY BOOKS FOR THE COMPANY OF CAPT. JOHN BLISS. 1813-14. 2 vols.
   (Nos. 231/90A; 233/90C). 1 in.   200
     Arranged by time period and thereunder by type of record.

COMPANY BOOK FOR THE COMPANY OF CAPT. WILLIAM S. FOSTER. 1814-15.
   1 vol. (No. 235/92). 1 in.   201
     Arranged by type of record. List of contents.

COMPANY BOOK FOR THE COMPANY OF CAPTS. VALENTINE R. GOODRICH AND
   JOHN BLISS. 1812-14. 1 vol. (No. 232/90B). 1/2 in.   202
     Arranged by type of record.

COMPANY BOOK FOR THE COMPANY OF CAPT. SAMUEL GORDON. 1812-13.
   1 vol. (No. 161/-). 1/2 in.   203
     Arranged by type of record. Name index.

COMPANY BOOK FOR THE COMPANY OF CAPTS. JOSEPH GRISWOLD AND WILLIAM
   S. FOSTER. 1812-15. 1 vol. (No. 229/87). 1 in.   204
     Arranged by type of record.

COMPANY BOOK FOR THE COMPANY OF CAPT. BENJAMIN SMEAD. 1812-15.
   1 vol. (No. 230/88). 1 in.   205
     Arranged by type of record.

COMPANY BOOK FOR THE COMPANY OF CAPT. JOHN W. WEEKS. 1812-14.
   1 vol. (No. 227/86). 1 in.   206
     Arranged by type of record.

COMPANY BOOK FOR THE COMPANY OF CAPTS. JOHN W. WEEKS AND MALACHI
   CORNING. 1814. 1 vol. (No. 228/86). 1 in.   207
     Arranged by type of record.

1. <u>12th (1812-15) Regiment, 1812-15</u>

ORDERLY BOOK FOR THE COMPANY OF CAPT. A. L. MADISON. Dec. 1813-
    Aug. 1814. 1 vol. (No. 243/98B). 1/2 in.   <u>208</u>
    Arranged in two chronological subseries: (1) Northern Army
general orders and brigade orders received, and (2) regimental and
detachment orders received. Also contains regimental orders issued
by the 6th Infantry, Dec. 1813-Mar. 1814.

COMPANY BOOK FOR THE COMPANY OF CAPTS. JAMES CHARLTON AND THOMAS
    SANGSTER. 1813-15. 1 vol. (No. 240/96). 1 in.   <u>209</u>
    Arranged by type of record. Contains a few regimental orders and
Division orders received, Aug.-Sept. 1814 and May 1815.

COMPANY BOOK FOR THE COMPANY OF CAPT. ANDREW L. MADISON. 1812-15.
    1 vol. (No.242/98A). 1 in.   <u>210</u>
    Arranged by type of record.

COMPANY BOOK FOR THE COMPANY OF CAPT. THOMAS P. MOORE. 1813-14.
    1 vol. (No. 244/99A). 1 in.   <u>211</u>
    Arranged by type of record.

COMPANY BOOK FOR THE COMPANY OF CAPT. JAMES PAXTON. 1812-15.
    1 vol. (No. 239/95). 1 in.   <u>212</u>
    Arranged by type of record.

COMPANY BOOK FOR THE COMPANY OF CAPT. THOMAS POST. 1813-15.
    1 vol. (No. 236/93A). 1 in.   <u>213</u>
    Arranged by type of record. Name index.

CLOTHING BOOK FOR THE COMPANY OF CAPT. THOMAS POST. 1814-15.
    1 vol. (No. 237/93B). 1 in.   <u>214</u>
    Arranged by name of individual. Name index.

COMPANY BOOK FOR THE COMPANY OF CAPT. THOMAS SANGSTER. 1815.
    1 vol. (No. 241/97). 1 in.   <u>215</u>
    Arranged by type of record.

COMPANY BOOK FOR THE COMPANY OF CAPT. LEWIS B. WILLIS. 1814-15.
    1 vol. (No. 245/99B). 1 in.   <u>216</u>
    Arranged by type of record.

m. <u>13th (1812-15) Regiment, 1813-15</u>

COMPANY BOOK FOR THE COMPANY OF CAPT. WILLIAM B. ADAMS. 1814-15.
    1 vol. (No. 247/101). 2 in.   <u>217</u>
    Arranged by type of record. Name index.

COMPANY BOOK FOR THE COMPANY OF CAPT. MYNDERT M. DOX. 1813-15.
   1 vol. (No. 246/100). 1 in.   218
   Arranged by type of record.

COMPANY BOOKS FOR THE COMPANY OF CAPT. STEPHEN W. KEARNY. 1814-15.
   2 vols. (Nos. 251/105A; 252/105B). 2 in.   219
   Arranged by year and thereunder by type of record. Name indexes.
Volume 251 also contains regimental and Northern Army orders received,
May-Oct. 1814.

COMPANY BOOK FOR THE COMPANY OF CAPT.MORDECAI MEYER. 1814-15.
   1 vol. (No. 249/103). 1 in.   220
   Arranged by type of record.

COMPANY BOOK FOR THE COMPANY OF CAPT. JOHN K. PAIGE. 1814-15.
   1 vol. (No. 248/102). 1 in.   221
   Arranged by type of record.

n.   14th (1812-15) Regiment, 1812-15

COMPANY BOOK FOR THE COMPANY OF CAPT. SAMUEL LANE. 1812-15. 1 vol.
   (No. 253/106). 1 in.   222
   Arranged by type of record.

o.   16th (1812-15) Regiment, 1813-15

COMPANY BOOK FOR THE COMPANY OF CAPTS. JONATHAN W. AITKEN AND
   THOMAS HORRELL. 1814-15. 1 vol. (No. 261/112B). 1 in.   223
   Arranged by type of record.

COMPANY BOOK FOR THE COMPANY OF CAPTS. JOHN BALDY AND THOMAS
   HORRELL. 1814-15. 1 vol. (No. 260/112A). 1 in.   224
   Arranged by type of record.

COMPANY BOOKS FOR THE COMPANY OF CAPT. WILLIAM DAVENPORT. 1813-15.
   2 vols. (Nos. 256/109A; 257/109B). 2 in.   225
   Arranged by time period and thereunder by type of record. Name
index to clothing accounts in volume 257.

COMPANY BOOK FOR THE COMPANY OF CAPT. JAMES F. McELROY. 1814-15.
   1 vol. (No. 255/108). 1 in.   226
   Arranged by type of record. Name index.

COMPANY BOOK FOR THE COMPANY OF CAPT. NATHANIEL McLAUGHLIN. 1814-15.
   1 vol. (No. 259/111). 1 in.   227
   Arranged by type of record.

COMPANY BOOK FOR THE COMPANY OF LT.. THOMAS M. POWERS. 1813-15.
   1 vol. (No. 258/110). 1 in.   228
   Arranged by type of record. Name index.

p. 18th (1812-15) Regiment, 1814-15

COMPANY BOOK FOR THE COMPANY OF CAPT. ROBERT FENNER. 1814-15.
   1 vol. (684/-). 1 in.   229
   Arranged by type of record.

q. 20th (1812-15) Regiment, 1812-14

COMPANY BOOK FOR THE COMPANY OF CAPT. WILLIAM S. JETT. 1812-14.
   1 vol. (No. 264/115). 1 in.   230
   Arranged by type of record.

COMPANY BOOK FOR THE COMPANY OF CAPTS. JOHN STANARD AND JOHN
   MACRAE. 1812-14. 1 vol. (No. 262/113). 1 in.   231
   Arranged by type of record. Name index.

COMPANY BOOK FOR THE COMPANY OF CAPT. BYRD C. WILLIS. 1813-14.
   1 vol. (No. 263/114). 1 in.   232
   Arranged by type of record.

r. 21st (1812-15) Regiment, 1812-15

COMPANY BOOK FOR THE COMPANY OF CAPT. LEMUEL BRADFORD. 1812-15.
   2 vols. (Nos. 265/46; 271/123A). 1 in.   233
   Arranged by type of record.

COMPANY BOOK FOR THE COMPANY OF CAPTS. LEMUEL BRADFORD AND IRA
   DREW. 1814-15. 1 vol. (No. 272/123B). 1 in.   234
   Arranged by type of record. List of contents.

COMPANY BOOK FOR THE COMPANY OF CAPT. SULLIVAN BURBANK. 1814.
   1 vol. (No. 268/120). 1 in.   235
   Arranged by type of record. List of contents.

LETTERS SENT AND ORDERS SENT AND RECEIVED BY CAPT. JEREMIAH CHAPMAN,
   COMMANDING THE RECRUITING DISTRICT UNDER THE BOSTON RENDEZVOUS.
   Apr. 1812-Feb. 1813. 1 vol. (No. 267/119). 1 in.   236
   Arranged chronologically. Also contains monthly returns of the
recruiting party commanded by Captain Chapman, 1812-13.

COMPANY BOOK FOR THE COMPANY OF CAPT. MORRILL MARSTON. 1813-14.
   1 vol. (No. 266/118). 1 in.   237
   Arranged by type of record. Name and subject index.

COMPANY BOOK FOR THE COMPANY OF CAPT. CHARLES PROCTER. 1813-15.
   1 vol. (No. 269/121). 2 in.   <u>238</u>
   Arranged by type of record. Name index.

COMPANY BOOKS FOR THE COMPANY OF CAPT. JOSEPH TREAT. 1813-15.
   2 vols. (Nos. 99/122B; 270/122A). 2 in.   <u>239</u>
   Arranged by type of record. Name index in first volume.

COMPANY BOOK FOR THE COMPANY OF CAPT. JOSIAH H. VOSE. 1813-14.
   1 vol. (No. 364/117). 1 in.   <u>240</u>
   Arranged by type of record.

s. <u>22d (1812-15) Regiment</u>, 1812-15

COMPANY BOOK FOR THE COMPANY OF CAPT. GEORGE W. BARKER AND LT.
   THOMAS Y. SPROGELL. 1813. 1 vol. (No. 275/125). 1 in.   <u>241</u>
   Arranged by type of record.

COMPANY BOOK FOR THE COMPANY OF CAPT. JACOB CARMACK. 1814-15.
   1 vol. (No. 281/130). 1 in.   <u>242</u>
   Arranged by type of record. Name index.

COMPANY BOOK FOR THE COMPANY OF CAPT. WILLIS FOULK. 1813-15.
   1 vol. (No. 277/127). 1 in.   <u>243</u>
   Arranged by type of record. List of contents and name index.

COMPANY BOOK FOR THE COMPANY OF CAPT. JOSEPH HENDERSON. 1813-15.
   1 vol. (No. 280/129). 3 in.   <u>244</u>
   Arranged by type of record.

COMPANY BOOKS FOR THE COMPANY OF CAPT. THOMAS LAWRENCE. 1814-15.
   2 vols. (Nos. 278/128A; 279/128B). 2 in.   <u>245</u>
   Arranged by time period and thereunder by type of record. Name
index in volume 278; list of contents in volume 279.

COMPANY BOOK FOR THE COMPANY OF CAPTS. DAVID MILLIKEN AND DANIEL
   McFARLAND. 1812-13. 1 vol. (No. 276/126). 1 in.   <u>246</u>
   Arranged by type of record. Name index.

COMPANY BOOKS FOR THE COMPANY OF CAPT. JOHN PENTLAND. 1812-14.
   2 vols. (Nos. 273/124A; 274/124B). 3 in.   <u>247</u>
   Arranged by time period and thereunder by type of record. Name
indexes.

t. 23d (1812-15) Regiment, 1814-15

COMPANY BOOK FOR THE COMPANY OF CAPT. FREDERICK BROWN. 1814-15.
1 vol. (No. 284/133). 1 in.   248
    Arranged by type of record.

COMPANY BOOK FOR THE COMPANY OF CAPT. RICHARD GOODELL. 1814.
1 vol. (No. 283/132). 1 in.   249
    Arranged by type of record. List of contents.

COMPANY BOOK FOR THE COMPANY OF LT. JUSTUS INGERSOLL. 1814-15.
1 vol. (No. 282/131). 1 in.   250
    Arranged by type of record.

COMPANY BOOK FOR THE COMPANY OF CAPTS. AZARIAH W. ODELL AND LT.
WILLIAM G. BELKNAP. 1814-15. 1 vol. (No. 285/134). 1/2 in.   251
    Arranged by type of record. List of contents.

u. 25th (1812-15) Regiment, 1812-15

COMPANY BOOKS FOR THE COMPANY OF CAPTS. JESSE BEACH AND DANIEL
KETCHUM. 1814-15. 2 vols. (Nos. 292/141; 294/143). 3 in.   252
    Arranged by time period and thereunder by type of record. List
of contents and name index in volume 292.

COMPANY BOOK FOR THE COMPANY OF CAPT. PETER BRADLEY. 1813-14.
1 vol. (No. 291/140). 1 in.   253
    Arranged by type of record.

COMPANY BOOK FOR THE COMPANY OF CAPTS. FESTUS CONE AND THOMAS M.
READ. 1812-14. 1 vol. (No. 288/137). 1 in.   254
    Arranged by type of record.

COMPANY BOOK FOR THE COMPANY OF CAPT. ARCHIBALD C. CRARY. 1814-15.
1 vol. (No. 293/142). 1 in.   255
    Arranged by type of record. List of contents.

COMPANY BOOK FOR THE COMPANY OF CAPT. GEORGE HOWARD. 1812-13.
1 vol. (No. 286/135). 1 in.   256
    Arranged by type of record. Name index.

COMPANY BOOK FOR THE COMPANY OF CAPT. THOMAS S. SEYMOUR. 1814-15.
1 vol. (No. 287/136). 1 in.   257
    Arranged by type of record. Name index.

COMPANY BOOK FOR THE COMPANY OF CAPT. EDWARD WHITE. 1814-15.
  1 vol. (No. 290/139). 2 in.   258
  Arranged by type of record. Name index.

REGISTER OF CLOTHING, ARMS, AND AMMUNITION ISSUED TO COMPANY OF
  CAPTS. BENJAMIN WATSON AND JAMES BURBIDGE. 1814-15. 1 vol.
  (No. 289/138). 3 in.   259
  Arranged by name of soldier. Also contains weekly returns of the
recruiting party commanded by Capt. Wilson Elliott, 19th Infantry,
July-Aug. 1812.

v. 26th (1814-15) Regiment, 1814-15

COMPANY BOOK FOR THE COMPANY OF CAPT. ELIJAH BOARDMAN. 1814-15.
  1 vol. (No. 295/144). 1 in.   260
  Arranged by type of record. Name index.

COMPANY BOOK FOR THE COMPANY OF CAPT. IRA WILLIAMS. 1814-15.
  1 vol. (No. 297/146). 1 in.   261
  Arranged by type of record. Name index. Contains company and
detachment orders issued by Capt. Williams.

COMPANY BOOK FOR THE COMPANY OF CAPTS. JOHN LEVAKE AND SALMON C.
  COTTON. 1814-15. 1 vol. (No. 296/145). 1 in.   262
  Arranged by type of record.

w. 27th (1814-15) Regiment, 1814-15

COMPANY BOOK FOR THE COMPANY OF CAPT. AARON T. CRANE. 1814-15.
  1 vol. (No. 298/147). 1 in.   263
  Arranged by type of record.

COMPANY BOOK FOR THE COMPANY OF CAPT. THOMAS EARLE. 1814-15.
  1 vol. (No. 300/149). 1 in.   264
  Arranged by type of record. Name index.

ORDERLY BOOK AND COMPANY BOOK FOR THE COMPANY OF CAPT. CHRISTIAN
  HARTELL. 1814-15. 1 vol. (No. 299/148). 1 in.   265
  Arranged by orders and company book information; orders arranged
thereunder chronologically, and company book information arranged
thereunder by type of record. The orders are 3d Military District
General Orders and regimental and brigade orders.

COMPANY BOOK FOR THE COMPANY OF CAPT. JAMES PORTER. 1814-15.
  1 vol. (No. 301/150). 1 in.   266
  Arranged by type of record. Name index.

COMPANY BOOK FOR THE COMPANY OF CAPT. ALLEN REYNOLDS. 1814-15.
    1 vol. (No. 302/151). 1 in.   267
    Arranged by type of record. List of contents.

COMPANY BOOK FOR THE COMPANY OF CAPT. BENJAMIN F. WOOD. 1814-15.
    1 vol. (No. 303/152). 1 in.   268
    Arranged by type of record.

x.   29th (1813-15) Regiment, 1813-15

COMPANY BOOK FOR THE COMPANY OF CAPT. JOHN C. ROCHESTER. 1813-15.
    1 vol. (No. 305/154). 1 in.   269
    Arranged by type of record.

COMPANY BOOK FOR THE COMPANY OF CAPT. JAMES B. SPENCER. 1814-15.
    1 vol. (No. 304/153). 1/2 in.   270
    Arranged by type of record. List of contents and name index.

COMPANY BOOK FOR THE COMPANY OF CAPT. PETER B. VAN BUREN. 1813-15.
    1 vol. (No. 306/155). 1 in.   271
    Arranged by type of record. List of contents and name index.

y.   30th (1813-15) Regiment, 1813-15

COMPANY BOOK FOR THE COMPANY OF CAPT. WILLIAM MILLER. 1813-15.
    1 vol. (No. 307/156). 1 in.   272
    Arranged by type of record.

COMPANY BOOK FOR THE COMPANY OF CAPT. DAVID SANFORD. 1814-15.
    1 vol. (No. 308/157). 1 in.   273
    Arranged by type of record.

COMPANY BOOK FOR THE COMPANY OF CAPT. JAMES TAYLOR. 1815.
    1 vol. (No. 309/158). 1 in.   274
    Arranged by type of record.

z.   31st (1813-15) Regiment, 1814-15

COMPANY BOOK FOR THE COMPANY OF CAPT. ANDREW ARNOLD. 1814-15.
    1 vol. (No. 312/161). 1 in.   275
    Arranged by type of record.

COMPANY BOOK FOR THE COMPANY OF CAPT. ETHAN BURNAP. 1814-15.
    1 vol. (No. 310/159). 1 in.   276
    Arranged by type of record. List of contents.

COMPANY BOOK FOR THE COMPANY OF CAPT. RUFUS STEWART. 1814-15.
    1 vol. (No. 311/160). 1 in.   277
    Arranged by type of record.

        aa. <u>32d (1813-15) Regiment, 1813-15</u>

COMPANY BOOK FOR THE COMPANY OF CAPT. SAMUEL BORDEN. 1813-15.
    1 vol. (No. 313/162). 2 in.   278
    Arranged by type of record. Name index.

COMPANY BOOK FOR THE COMPANY OF CAPT. JOHN STEELE, JR. 1814-15.
    1 vol. (No. 314/163). 1 in.   279
    Arranged by type of record.

ORDERLY AND COMPANY BOOK FOR THE COMPANY OF CAPT. GEORGE F. GOODMAN.
    1814-15. 1 vol. (No. 315/164). 1 in.   280
    Arranged by orders and company book information; orders arranged
thereunder chronologically, and company book information arranged
thereunder by type of record. The orders are War Department and 3d
Military District General Orders and garrison orders of New Utrecht,
Sandy Hook, and Fort Columbus. Also includes a few letters received.

        bb. <u>33d (1813-15) Regiment, 1814-15</u>

COMPANY BOOK FOR THE COMPANY OF CAPT. JAMES CURRY. 1814-15.
    1 vol. (No. 317/166). 1 in.   281
    Arranged by type of record. List of contents.

COMPANY BOOK FOR THE COMPANY OF CAPT. BENJAMIN DUNN. 1814-15.
    1 vol. (No. 316/165). 1 in.   282
    Arranged by type of record.

        cc. <u>34th (1813-15) Regiment, 1814-15</u>

COMPANY BOOK FOR THE COMPANY OF CAPT. THOMAS BAILEY. 1814-15.
    1 vol. (No. 320/169). 1 in.   283
    Arranged by type of record.

COMPANY BOOK FOR THE COMPANY OF CAPT. ISAAC CARTER. 1814-15.
    1 vol. (No. 321/170). 1/2 in.   284
    Arranged by type of record.

COMPANY BOOK FOR THE COMPANY OF CAPT. PETER CHADWICK. 1814-15.
    1 vol. (No. 319/168). 1/2 in.   285
    Arranged by type of record.

COMPANY BOOK FOR THE COMPANY OF CAPT. ROBERT R. KENDALL. 1814-15.
     1 vol. (No. 318/167). 1/2 in.   286
     Arranged by type of record. List of contents.

COMPANY BOOK FOR THE COMPANY OF CAPT. BENJAMIN POLAND. 1814-15.
     1 vol. (No. 322/171). 1 in.   287
     Arranged by type of record.

          dd. 35th (1813-15) Regiment, 1814-15

COMPANY BOOK FOR THE COMPANY OF CAPT. WALTER T. COCKE. 1814-15.
     1 vol. (No. 323/172). 1 in.   288
     Arranged by type of record. Name index.

COMPANY BOOK FOR THE COMPANY OF CAPT. FRANCIS E. WALKER. 1814-15.
     1 vol. (No. 324/173). 2 in.   289
     Arranged by type of record.

          ee. 37th (1813-15) Regiment, 1813-15

COMPANY BOOK FOR THE COMPANY OF CAPT. JOHN BROWN. 1814-15.
     1 vol. (No. 329/178). 1 in.   290
     Arranged by type of record.

COMPANY BOOK FOR THE COMPANY OF CAPTS. CHAUNCEY IVES AND DAVID T.
     WELCH. 1813-15. 1 vol. (No. 330/179). 1 in.   291
     Arranged by type of record. List of contents.

COMPANY BOOK FOR THE COMPANY OF CAPT. SAMUEL B. NORTHROP. 1813-15.
     1 vol. (No. 328/177). 1/2 in.   292
     Arranged by type of record.

COMPANY BOOK FOR THE COMPANY OF CAPT. CHRISTOPHER RIPLEY. 1813-15.
     1 vol. (No. 325/174). 1 in.   293
     Arranged by type of record. Name index.

COMPANY BOOK FOR THE COMPANY OF CAPT. STEPHEN D. TILDEN. 1814-15.
     1 vol. (No. 327/176). 1/2 in.   294
     Arranged by type of record.

COMPANY BOOK FOR THE COMPANY OF CAPT. ELIZUR WARNER. 1813-15.
     1 vol. (No. 326/175). 2 in.   295
     Arranged by type of record. Name index.

COMPANY BOOK FOR THE COMPANY OF CAPT. WILLIAM S. RADCLIFF. 1814-15.
    1 vol. (No. 338/187). 1 in.   306
    Arranged by type of record.

COMPANY BOOK FOR THE COMPANY OF CAPT. GILBERT SEAMAN. 1814-15.
    1 vol. (No. 339/188). 1 in.   307
    Arranged by type of record.

COMPANY BOOK FOR THE COMPANY OF CAPT. ALPHEUS SHERMAN. 1814-15.1 vol.
    (No. 335/184). 1 in.   308
    Arranged by type of record.

ii. 42nd (1813-15) Regiment, 1813-15

COMPANY BOOK FOR THE COMPANY OF CAPT. GEORGE W. BARKER. 1814-15.
    1 vol. (No. 344/193). 1 in.   309
    Arranged by type of record.

COMPANY BOOK FOR THE COMPANY OF CAPT. JOHN BIDDLE. 1813-15.
    1 vol. (No. 346/194B). 1 in.   310
    Arranged by type of record.

COMPANY BOOK FOR THE COMPANY OF CAPTS. JOHN BIDDLE AND THOMAS
    HANSON. 1814-15. 1 vol. (No. 345/194A). 1 in.   311
    Arranged by type of record.

COMPANY BOOK FOR THE COMPANY OF CAPT. JAMES F. DE PEYSTER. 1814-15.
    1 vol. (No. 342/191). 1/2 in.   312
    Arranged by type of record. List of contents.

COMPANY BOOK FOR THE COMPANY OF CAPT. EDMUND B. DUVAL. 1814-15.
    1 vol. (No. 343/192). 1 in.   313
    Arranged by type of record. List of contents.

jj. 43d (1813-15) Regiment, 1814-15

COMPANY BOOK FOR THE COMPANY OF CAPT. GEORGE DABNEY. 1814-15.
    1 vol. (No. 348/196). 1/2 in.   314
    Arranged by type of record.

kk. 45th (1814-15) Regiment, 1814-15

COMPANY BOOK FOR THE COMPANY OF CAPT. SMITH ELKINS. 1814. 1 vol.
    (No. 28/199). 1 in.   315
    Arranged by type of record. List of contents.

COMPANY BOOK FOR THE COMPANY OF CAPT. JOSEPH FLANDERS. 1814-15.
    1 vol. (No. 27/198). 1 in.   316
    Arranged by type of record. Name and subject index.

COMPANY BOOK FOR THE COMPANY OF CAPT. DANIEL M. GREGG. 1814-15.
    1 vol. (No. 349/197). 1 in.   317
    Arranged by type of record. List of contents and name index.

COMPANY BOOK FOR THE COMPANY OF CAPT. DANIEL HOLDEN. 1814-15.
    1 vol. (No. 29/200). 1/2 in.   318
    Arranged by type of record.

11. 46th (1814-15) Regiment, 1814-15

COMPANY BOOK FOR THE COMPANY OF CAPT. MOSES D. BURNETT. 1814-15.
    1 vol. (No. 31/202). 1 in.   319
    Arranged by type of record.

COMPANY BOOK FOR THE COMPANY OF CAPT. PETER MILLER. 1814-15.
    1 vol. (No. 32/203). 1 in.   320
    Arranged by type of record. List of contents.

COMPANY BOOK FOR THE COMPANY OF CAPT. JOB WRIGHT. 1814-15. 1 vol.
    (No. 30/201). 1/2 in.   321
    Arranged by type of record.

mm. Maj. Zebulon M. Pike's Consolidated Regiment, 1809-11

On April 11, 1810, pursuant to a General Order of February 28, 1810,
10 companies of the 3d and 5th Infantry Regiments were consolidated into
the regiment of infantry at Cantonment Washington under the command of
Maj. Zebulon M. Pike. By March 1811 this consolidated regiment had
moved to Baton Rouge.

ORDERLY BOOK FOR THE COMPANY OF CAPTS. MOSSMAN HOUSTON AND WILLIAM R.
    DAVIS, 3D INFANTRY. Nov. 1809-May 1810. 1 vol. (No. 387/271).
    1 in.   322
    Arranged chronologically. This company was stationed at Camp
Natchez, Miss., in Nov. 1809 and thereafter at Cantonment Washington,
Miss.

ORDERLY BOOK OF THE ADJUTANT. July-Nov. 1810. 1 vol. (No. 388/272).
    1 in.   323
    Arranged chronologically.

ORDERLY BOOK FOR THE COMPANY OF CAPT. JOHN DARRINGTON, 3D INFANTRY.
    Mar.-May 1811. 1 vol. (No. 430/327). 1 in.   <u>324</u>
    Arranged chronologically. At the back of the volume are a few
orders of Captain Butler's Company, 3d Infantry, which was not a part
of the consolidated regiment.

ORDERLY BOOK FOR THE COMPANY OF CAPT. JAMES E. DINKINS, 3D INFANTRY.
    Mar.-Nov. 1811. 1 vol. (No. 503/405). 1 in.   <u>325</u>
    Arranged chronologically.

3. Records Relating to the 1815-21 Period

a. 1st (1815-?) Regiment, 1815-21

Unless otherwise stated, the companies of the 1st Regiment whose
orderly books are described below were at the following stations:

    June 1815-Dec. 1815 Pass Christian, Miss.
    Dec. 1815-June 1816 New Orleans, La.
    June 1816-Oct. 1816 Baton Rouge, La.
    ****
    Feb. 1817-Dec. 1817 Baton Rouge, La.
    Dec. 1817-Apr. 1818 New Orleans, La.
    Apr. 1818-May 1821   Baton Rouge, La.

(1). Orderly Books

From 1815 to 1821 the 1st Infantry Regiment was in the 8th Mili-
tary Department. Therefore, the orderly books will normally contain
War Department, Division of the South, and 8th Military Department
General Orders, as well as garrison and regimental orders.

WAR DEPARTMENT, DIVISION OF THE SOUTH, AND 8TH MILITARY DEPARTMENT
    GENERAL ORDERS RECEIVED. Sept. 1816-Apr. 1819. 1 vol.
    (No. 450/348). 2 in.   <u>326</u>
    Arranged chronologically.

ORDERLY BOOKS FOR THE COMPANY OF CAPT. FERDINAND AMELUNG. July
    1817-Mar. 1820; May 1821-Apr. 1822. 3 vols. (Nos. 489/390;
    76/223; 476/377). 3 in.   <u>327</u>
    Arranged chronologically. Amelung's Company was on detached duty
at Forts Claiborne and Selden, La., and Camp Ripley from Jan. 1819 to
Mar. 1820.

ORDERLY BOOKS FOR THE COMPANY OF CAPT. ISAAC BAKER. July 1815-May 1816;
    Feb.-Aug. 1817. 2 vols. (Nos. 500/402; 502/404). 2 in.   <u>328</u>
    Arranged chronologically.

ORDERLY BOOK FOR THE COMPANY OF CAPT. WILLIAM BUTLER DETAILED UNDER
THE COMMAND OF CAPT. RICHARD CALL. Nov. 1816-June 1817. 1 vol.
(No. 432/329). 1 in.   329
    Arranged chronologically. Butler's Company was detailed to Fort
Bowyer, Ala., during this period.

ORDERLY BOOKS FOR THE COMPANY OF CAPT. WILLIAM CHRISTIAN. June 1815-
Oct. 1816; Jan. 1817-Mar. 1818. 3 vols. (Nos. 479/380; 66/213;
69/216). 3 in.   330
    Arranged chronologically. Christian's Company was detailed to cut
public roads near Covington, La., in 1817.

ORDERLY BOOK FOR THE COMPANY OF CAPT. ROBERT L. COOMB. July 1820-
Sept. 1821. 1 vol. (No. 400/283). 1/2 in.   331
    Arranged chronologically. Capt. Coomb was in charge of the post
of Natchitoches, La., and its dependencies.

ORDERLY BOOKS FOR THE COMPANY OF CAPT. JOHN JONES. Jan.-May 1817;
Aug. 1817-Sept. 1819. 3 vols. (No. 68/215; 71/218; 75/222).
3 in.   332
    Arranged chronologically. Jones' Company was on detached duty at
Nova Iberia, La., from Feb. to Apr. 1817 and at or near Fort Barrancas,
Fla., from May to Oct. 1818.

ORDERLY BOOK FOR THE COMPANY OF CAPT. WILLIAM LAVAL DETAILED UNDER THE
COMMAND OF CAPT. ROBERT COOMB. Feb.-Dec. 1816. 1 vol.
(No. 436/333). 1 in.   333
    Arranged chronologically. Laval's Company was on detail to Petite
Coquille, La., from May to Dec. 1816.

ORDERLY BOOKS FOR THE COMPANY OF CAPT. WILLIAM LAVAL. Jan. 1818-
Aug. 1820. 2 vols. (Nos. 74/221; 483/384). 2 in.   334
    Arranged chronologically. Laval's Company was on detached duty
at Forts Claiborne and Selden, La., and Camp Ripley from Jan. 1819
to Dec. 1820.

ORDERLY BOOK FOR THE COMPANY OF CAPT. JOSEPH MILES. Feb.-Sept. 1817.
1 vol. (No. 434/331). 1 in.   335
    Arranged generally chronologically. Miles' Company was detailed to
cut public roads in 1817 near Covington, La.

ORDERLY BOOK FOR THE COMPANY OF CAPT. ANATOLE PEYCHAUD. Oct. 1817-
July 1820. 2 vols. (Nos. 469/368; 78/225). 2 in.   336
    Arranged generally chronologically. Peychaud's Company was part
of the second detachment detailed to cut public roads near Covington,
La., late in 1817.

ORDERLY BOOK FOR THE COMPANY OF CAPT. WILLIAM SUMTER. Oct. 1817-
Apr. 1819. 1 vol. (No. 70/217). 1 in.   <u>337</u>
Arranged chronologically. Sumter's Company was part of the second
detachment detailed to cut public roads near Covington, La., late in
1817.

ORDERLY BOOKS OF AN UNIDENTIFIED COMPANY. Aug. 1815-Oct. 1816.
2 vols. (Nos. 481/382; 478/379). 2 in.   <u>338</u>
Arranged chronologically.

ORDERLY BOOK OF AN UNIDENTIFIED COMPANY. Nov. 1815-July 1816.
1 vol. (No. 505/407). 1 in.   <u>339</u>
Arranged chronologically.

ORDERLY BOOKS OF AN UNIDENTIFIED COMPANY. Jan. 1818-May 1821.
3 vols. (Nos. 73/220; 79/226; 83/230). 4 in.   <u>340</u>
Arranged chronologically.

ORDERLY BOOK OF AN UNIDENTIFIED COMPANY. Dec. 1818-Apr. 1820.
1 vol. (No. 77/224). 1 in.   <u>341</u>
Arranged chronologically.

ORDERLY BOOK OF AN UNIDENTIFIED COMPANY. Dec. 1819-May 1821.
1 vol. (No. 80/227). 1 in.   <u>342</u>
Arranged chronologically.

ORDERLY BOOK OF AN UNIDENTIFIED COMPANY. Jan. 1821-July 1821.
1 vol. (No.81/228). 2 in.   <u>343</u>
Arranged chronologically.

ORDERLY BOOK OF AN UNIDENTIFIED COMPANY. Feb. 1820-Apr. 1821.
1 vol. (No. 82/229). 1 in.   <u>344</u>
Arranged in two chronological subseries: (1) Department and general orders received and (2) garrison and regimental orders.

(2). Company Books

COMPANY BOOK FOR THE COMPANY OF CAPT. FERDINAND AMELUNG. 1815-18.
1 vol. (No. 57/45). 1 in.   <u>345</u>
Arranged by type of record.

COMPANY BOOK FOR THE COMPANY OF CAPT. HENRY CHOTARD. 1815-18.
1 vol. (No. 56/44). 1 in.   <u>346</u>
Arranged by type of record.

COMPANY BOOK FOR THE COMPANY OF CAPTS. HENRY CHOTARD AND JOHN JONES.
    1819-21. 1 vol. (No. 62/49). 1 in.   <u>347</u>
    Arranged by type of record.

COMPANY RECEIPT BOOK FOR THE COMPANY OF CAPT. WILLIAM CHRISTIAN.
    1817-19. 1 vol. (No. 72/219). 1/2 in.   <u>348</u>
    Arranged chronologically.

COMPANY BOOK FOR THE COMPANY OF CAPTS. WILLIAM KER, TRUEMAN CROSS,
    AND THOMAS F. SMITH. 1816-21. 1 vol. (No. 63/50). 1 in. <u>349</u>
    Arranged by type of record. Name index.

COMPANY BOOK FOR THE COMPANY OF CAPT. JOHN JONES. 1817-19.
    1 vol. (No. 58/46). 1/2 in.   <u>350</u>
    Arranged by type of record. Name index.

COMPANY BOOKS FOR THE COMPANY OF CAPT. WILLIAM LAVAL. 1815-22.
    2 vols. (Nos. 60/48A; 61/48B). 2 in.   <u>351</u>
    Arranged by time period and thereunder by type of record. Name
indexes.

COMPANY BOOK FOR THE COMPANY OF CAPT. ANATOLE PEYCHAUD. 1817-18.
    1 vol. (No. 59/47). 1 in.   <u>352</u>
    Arranged by type of record.

COMPANY BOOK FOR THE BAND OF THE 1ST INFANTRY REGIMENT. 1817-21.
    1 vol. (No. 64/51A). 1 in.   <u>353</u>
    Arranged by type of record.

(3). Other Records

CLOTHING BOOKS. 1816-18. 2 vols. (1 n.n.; No. 138/440). 1 in. <u>354</u>
    Arranged chronologically. Volume 138/440 also contains guard re-
ports of the garrison at Baton Rouge, Sept.-Oct. 1823.

MORNING REPORTS OF TROOPS AT BATON ROUGE. Jan. 1818-July 1824.
    4 vols. (Nos. 89/429; 88/428; 86/426; 87/427). 5 in.   <u>355</u>
    Arranged chronologically.

b. <u>3d (1815-?) Regiment, 1820-21</u>

REGIMENTAL ORDERS ISSUED. 1820-21. 1 vol. 1 in.   <u>356</u>
    Arranged chronologically. Also contains guard reports, Jan.-Mar.
1827.

c. 7th (1815-?) Regiment, 1817-21

From 1817 to 1821 the 7th Regiment was under the 7th Military Department and the Division of the South.

ORDERLY BOOK OF THE FIRST LIGHT COMPANY. 1817-18. 1 vol.
   (No. 429/325). 1/2 in.   357
   Arranged chronologically.

ORDERLY BOOK. 1820-21. 1 vol. (No. 380/264). 1 in.   358
   Arranged chronologically.

d. 8th (1815-?) Regiment, 1818-21

From 1820 to 1821 the 8th Infantry was under the 8th Military Department and the Division of the South.

ORDERLY BOOK. 1820-21. 1 vol. (No. 381/265). 1 in.   359
  Arranged by "issued" and "received" and thereunder chronologically.

COMPANY BOOK FOR A DETACHMENT UNDER CAPT. WILLIAM DAVENPORT. 1818-21.
   1 vol. (No. 216/78). 1 in.   360
   Arranged by type of record. Name index.

COMPANY BOOK FOR THE COMPANY OF CAPTS. JOHN N. McINTOSH AND LEWIS
   B. WILLIS. 1819-21. 1 vol. (No. 215/77). 1 in.   361
   Arranged by type of record. Name index.

COMPANY BOOK FOR THE COMPANY OF CAPT. LEWIS B. WILLIS. 1819-21.
   1 vol. (No. 217/79). 1 in.   362
   Arranged by type of record. Also contains a company book for a
company of recruits under Lt. Wilson Whatley, 1818-19, arranged by
type of record. Name index to clothing and equipage issued.

CLOTHING ACCOUNTS BOOK. 1820-21. 1 vol. (No. 85/424). 1 in.   363
   Arranged alphabetically by initial letter of surname of soldier.

MORNING REPORTS. 1821. 1 vol. (No. 515/430). 1 in.   364
   Arranged chronologically.

D. Legion of the United States, 1792-93

The Legion existed from 1792 to 1796.

ORDERS ISSUED BY THE LEGION OF THE UNITED STATES AT PITTSBURGH AND
   LEGIONVILLE. Sept. 1792-Apr. 1793. 1 vol. (No. 499/401).
   1 in.   365
   Arranged chronologically.

CONSOLIDATED RETURNS OF ENLISTED MEN. 1789-92. 1 vol. 1/2 in.   366
      Arranged numerically by sub-legion, thereunder by company, and
thereunder chronologically.

    E. Riflemen

       1. 1st (1808-21) Regiment, 1812-15

ORDERLY BOOK FOR THE COMPANY OF CAPT. THOMAS RAMSEY. 1813-15.
   1 vol. (No. 501/403). 1 in.   367
   Arranged chronologically.

COMPANY BOOK FOR THE COMPANY OF CAPT. GEORGE GRAY. 1812-15.
   1 vol. (No. 201/33). 1 in.   368
   Arranged by type of record.

COMPANY BOOK FOR THE COMPANY OF CAPT. THOMAS RAMSEY. 1814-15.
   1 vol. (No. 202/34). 1 in.   369
   Arranged by type of record.

COMPANY BOOK FOR THE COMPANY OF CAPT. WILLIAM SMYTH AND LT. SAMUEL
   HAMILTON. 1813-15. 1 vol. (No. 200/32). 1 in.   370
   Arranged by type of record. List of contents.

COMPANY BOOK FOR THE COMPANY OF CAPT. EDWARD WADSWORTH. 1812-15.
   1 vol. (No. 199/31). 1 in.   371
   Arranged by type of record.

       2. 3d (1814-15) Regiment, 1814-15

COMPANY BOOK FOR THE COMPANY OF CAPTS. JOHN G. BLOUNT AND WM.
   DUFPHEY. 1814-15. 1 vol. (No. 206/38). 1/2 in.   372
   Arranged by type of record.

COMPANY BOOK FOR THE COMPANY OF CAPTS.ALEX. W. BRANDON AND WM. C.
   PARKER. 1814-15. 1 vol. (No. 203/35). 1 in.   373
   Arranged by type of record.

COMPANY BOOK FOR THE COMPANY OF CAPTS. JOHN E. CALHOUN AND WALTER
     COLES. 1814-15. 1 vol. (No. 207/39). 1/2 in.   374
     Arranged by type of record. Also contains 4th Military District
and regimental General Orders and other orders, Apr. 1815.

COMPANY BOOK FOR THE COMPANY OF CAPT. WYLY MARTIN. 1814-15. 1 vol.
     (No. 204/36). 1 in.   375
     Arranged by type of record.

MUSTER AND RECEIPT ROLLS FOR THE COMPANY OF CAPTS. THOMAS J. ROBESON
     AND WALTER COLES. 1814-15. 1 vol. (No. 205/37). 1 in.   376
     Arranged by type of roll. Also contains a Company Book for an
unidentified company of the 1st Artillery Regiment, 1811-14. Arranged
by type of record.

APPENDIX

List Showing Titles and Disposition of 689 Numbered Volumes of
Records Mainly of U.S. Army Commands, 1784-1821, in a Set
Constructed by the AGO; and a List of 27 Unnumbered Volumes of Similar Records Described in the Inventory
(see entry 2)

An asterisk (*) following volume numbers denotes volumes not described in this inventory. The disposition of such volumes is shown
in parentheses. Quoted titles or statements are those taken from the
original list in the absence of the volume itself. For the sake of
brevity, a number of familiar abbreviations are used. "Regiment" is
implied after numbered units such as "45th Inf."

A. List of 689 Numbered Volumes

Volumes   Title

 1-5*   Descriptive Rolls: Infantry, Rifles, Artillery. (In RG 94)
 6-11*   Muster Rolls. (In RG 94)
12-22*   Inspection Returns. (In RG 94)
  23*   Monthly Returns: Infantry. (In RG 94)
24-25*   Monthly Returns: Infantry, Artillery. (In RG 94).
  26   List of Officers and Men Received From the British in an
            Exchange of Men, 9th Mil. Dist. 1814.
  27   Company Book for Co. of Capt. Joseph Flanders, 45th Inf.
            1814-15.
  28   Company Book for Co. of Capt. Smith Elkins, 45th Inf. 1814.
  29   Company Book for Co. of Capt. Daniel Holden, 45th Inf.
            1814-15.
  30   Company Book for Co. of Capt. Job Wright, 46th Inf. 1814-15.
  31   Company Book for Co. of Capt. Moses D. Burnett, 46th Inf.
            1814-15.
  32   Company Book for Co. of Capt. Peter Miller, 46th Inf. 1814-15.
  33*   "Capt. Andrew Wilson's Co. Bk, 46th Inf. 1814-15." (Not Found)
  34*   "Capt. S. Ranney's Muster Rolls, 4th Inf. 1808-12." (Not Found)
  35*   Muster Rolls. (In RG 94)
  36   Monthly Returns, Light Art. 1816-19.
37-38*   Inspection Returns, Light Art. 1815-18. (In RG 94)
  39   Inspection Returns, Light Art. 1819-21.
  40   Register of Men Furloughed, 3d Mil. Dist. 1814-15.
  41   Miscellaneous Records, Light Art. 1811-21.
  42   Company Book for Co. of Capts. William Boote and William
            Lawrence, 2d Inf. 1812-14.

Volumes	Title

43* "Register of Officers, 5th Mil. Dept. 18.7-20." (Not Found)
44* "Militia General Returns, 1813-21." (Not Found)
45   Miscellaneous Returns of the Right and Left Divisions,9th
       Mil. Dist. 1813-15.
46* "Capt. Willis' Co. Book, 8th Inf. 1819-20." (Not Found)
47* "Capt. Perry's Co. Book, 40th Inf. 1813-15." (Not Found)
48-51* Monthly Returns: Infantry, Artillery, Districts. 1813-21.
       (In RG 94)
52   Company Book for Co. of Capt. Simon Owens, 1st Inf. 1810-14.
53   Company Book for Co. of Capts. John Symmes and Eli Clemson,
       1st Inf. 1807-15.
54   Company Book for Co. of Capts. Laurence Taliaferro and
       Linai T. Helm, 1st Inf. 1813-14.
55   Company Book for Co. of Capts. John Whistler and James Rhea,
       1st Inf. 1812-15.
56   Company Book for Co. of Capt. Henry Chotard, 1st Inf.
       1815-18.
57   Company Book for Co. of Capt. Ferdinand Amelung, 1st Inf.
       1815-18.
58   Company Book for Co. of Capt. John Jones, 1st Inf. 1817-19.
59   Company Book for Co. of Capt. Anatole Peychaud, 1st Inf.
       1817-18.
60   Company Book for Co. of Capt. William Laval, 1st Inf.
       1815-17.
61   Company Book for Co. of Capt. William Laval, 1st Inf.
       1817-22.
62   Company Book for Co. of Capts. Henry Chotard and John Jones,
       1st Inf. 1819-21.
63   Company Book for Co. of Capts. William Ker, Trueman Cross,
       and Thomas F. Smith, 1st Inf. 1816-21.
64   Company Book for the Band, 1st Inf. 1817-21.
65   Orderly Book for the Adjutant General, Division of the South.
       1817-21.
66   Orderly Book for the Co. of Capt. William Christian, 1st
       Inf. 1815-16.
67* "Orders, New Orleans, Baton Rouge, 1816-17." (Only cover
       found)
68   Orderly Book for Co. of Capt. John Jones, 1st Inf. 1817.
69   Orderly Book for Co. of Capt. William Christian, 1st Inf.
       1817-18.
70   Orderly Book for Co. of Capt. William Sumter, 1st Inf.
       1817-19.
71   Orderly Book for Co. of Capt. John Jones, 1st Inf. 1817-18.

Volumes	Title
72	Company Receipt Book for Co. of Capt. William Christian, 1st Inf. 1817-19.
73	Orderly Book for an Unidentified Co., 1st Inf. 1818-19.
74	Orderly Book for Co. of Capt. William Laval, 1st Inf. 1818-19.
75	Orderly Book for Co. of Capt. John Jones, 1st Inf. 1818-19.
76	Orderly Book for Co. of Capt. Ferdinand Amelung, 1st Inf. 1818-20.
77	Orderly Book for an Unidentified Co., 1st Inf. 1818-20.
78	Orderly Book for Co. of Capt. Anatole Peychaud, 1st Inf. 1819-20.
79	Orderly Book for an Unidentified Co., 1st Inf. 1819-20.
80	Orderly Book for an Unidentified Co., 1st Inf. 1819-21.
81	Orderly Book for an Unidentified Co., 1st Inf. 1821.
82	Orderly Book for an Unidentified Co., 1st Inf. 1820-21.
83	Orderly Book for an Unidentified Co., 1st Inf. 1820-21.
84*	"Orders, 1st Inf. Transf'd to Mr. Ellerbrook, Mch. 23/81." (Not found)
85	Clothing Accounts Book, 8th Inf. 1820-21.
86	Morning Reports of Troops at Baton Rouge, 1st Inf. 1822-23.
87	Morning Reports of Troops at Baton Rouge, 1st Inf. 1823-24.
88	Morning Reports of Troops at Baton Rouge, 1st Inf. 1821-22.
89	Morning Reports of Troops at Baton Rouge, 1st Inf. 1818-21.
90-91*	"Guard Reports, 1st Inf. Transf'd to Mr. Ellerbrook, Mch. 23/81." (Not found)
92	Reports Sent to the Secretary of War Relating to Cases of Militia Delinquents, Division of the North. 1818-19.
93*	General Returns, U.S. Army. 1801-21. (In RG 94)
94	Rosters of Noncommissioned Officers, 7th Inf. 1812-14.
95	Orderly Book, 7th Inf. 1814-15.
96	Orderly Book for Co. of Capt. Samuel Vail, 7th Inf. 1815.
97	Orderly Book for an Unidentified Co., 7th Inf. 1813-14.
98	Receipts for Clothing for Co. of Capt. Henry K. Craig, Light Art. 1817-19.
99	Company Book for Co. of Capt. Joseph Treat, 21st Inf. 1814-15.
100	Orderly Book for Co. of Capt. Richard Oldham, 7th Inf. 1814.
101*	"Guard Book, 1st Inf. Tf'd to Mr. Ellerbrook, Mch. 1881." (Not found)
102*	Yearly Tables of Numbers of Enlisted, Deserted, and Joined From Desertion. 1816-20. (In RG 94)
103	Registers of Discharges, Deaths, and Desertions; List of Officers; and Descriptive Rolls of Companies, 2d Inf. 1811-14.

Volumes	Title
104	Company Book for Co. of Capts. John Campbell and Robert Purdy, 2d Inf. 1803-7.
105	Company Book for Co. of Capts. John Campbell and John Luckett, 2d Inf. 1807-13.
106	Company Book for Co. of Capts. John Brahan and Reuben Chamberlain, 2d Inf. 1807-9.
107	Company Book for Co. of Capt. Reuben Chamberlain, 2d Inf. 1813-15.
108	Company Book for Co. of Capts. John Brahan and William Lawrence, 2d Inf. 1807-13.
109	Company Book for Co. of Capts. William Lawrence, Hezekiah Bradley, and Alexander Gray, 2d Inf. 1812-16.
110	Company Book for Co. of Capt. William R. Boote, 2d Inf. 1805-10.
111	Company Book for Co. of Capt. William R. Boote, 2d Inf. 1812-14.
112	Company Book for Co. of Capt. Richard Sparks, 2d Inf. 1802-5.
113	Orderly Book of an Unidentified Co. Stationed at New Orleans, 2d Inf. 1805-6.
114	Orderly Book of an Unidentified Co., 2d Inf. 1808.
115	Orderly Book for an Unidentified Co., 2d Inf. 1808-9
116	Orderly Book for an Unidentified Co., 2d Inf. 1809-10.
117	Orderly Book for an Unidentified Co., 2d Inf. 1809-10.
118	Orderly Book for Co. of Capt. William R. Boote, 2d Inf. 1810-12.
119	Orderly Book for an Unidentified Co., 2d Inf. 1810-11.
120	Orderly Book for Co. of Capt. Matthew Arbuckle, 2d Inf. 1812-13.
121	Morning Reports and Rosters for Co. of Capt. William Lawrence, 2d Inf. 1812.
122	Orderly Book for Co. of Capt. William Lawrence, 2d Inf. 1814-15.
123	Orderly Book for Co. of Capt. William Lawrence, 2d Inf. 1812-13.
124*	"Guard Rept. 1825. Tfd. to Mr. Ellerbrook, Mch. 1881." (Not found)
125	Register of Officers, 9th Mil. Dist. 1813-15.
126	Register of Officers, 9th Mil. Dist. 1814.
127	General Orders Received and District Orders Issued, 2d Mil. Dist. 1814-15.
128	Orderly Book for Co. of Capt. John L. Clark, 41st Inf. 1815.

Volumes	Title
129	Orderly Book of Capt. Richard Sparks, 2d Inf. 1803-4.
130	Orderly Book of an Unidentified Co., 2d Inf. 1810-11.
131-137*	"Transf'd to Mr. Ellerbrook, Mch. 23/81." (Not found)
138	Clothing Book, 1st Inf., 1817-18; Guard Reports, Baton Rouge, 1823.
139*	"Transfd to Mr. Ellerbrook, Mch. 23/81." (Not found)
140*	Monthly Returns: Infantry, 1816-21. (In RG 94)
141-146*	"Transf'd to Mr. Kirkley, Aug. 4/77." (Not found)
147-149*	"Not on file." (Not found)
150-152*	"Transf'd to Mr. Kirkley, Aug. 4/77." (Not found)
153	Company Book for Co. of Capt. Richard Sparks, 3d Inf. 1796-1800.
154	Company Book for Co. of Capt. Joseph Woodruff, 3d Inf. 1809-15.
155	Company Book for Co. of Capt. William Butler, 3d Inf. 1810-11.
156	Company Book for Co. of Capt. William Butler, 3d Inf. 1812-14.
157	Company Book for Co. of Capts. Samuel W. Butler, William Laval, and John McClelland, 3d Inf. 1812-15.
158	Company Book for Co. of Capts. Robert B. Moore and Henry Chotard, 3d Inf. 1812-15.
159	Company Book for Co. of Capt. Samuel C. Mabson, 3d Inf. 1812-15.
160	Company Book for Co. of Capt. James E. Dinkins, 3d Inf. 1812-15.
161	Company Book for Co. of Capt. Samuel Gordon, 11th Inf. 1812-13.
162	Orderly Book of Adjutant at Fort Adams, 3d Inf., 1801-2.; Orderly Book of Capt. Richard Sparks, 2d Inf., 1802-3.
163	Orderly Book for Co. of Capts. Joseph Woodruff and Samuel Mabson, 3d Inf. 1813-14.
164	Orderly Book for Co. of Capts. Joseph Woodruff and Samuel Mabson, 3d Inf. 1814.
165	Orderly Book for Co. of Capt. Samuel W. Butler, 3d Inf. 1815.
166	Company Book for Co. of Capt. William Littlejohn, 1st Dragoons. 1813-15.
167	Company Book for Co. of Capt. John A. Burd, 1st Dragoons. 1812-14.
168	Company Book for Co. of Capt. John A. Burd, 1st Dragoons, 1814-15.
169	Company Book for Co. of Capt. Luther Leonard, Light Art. 1812-15.
170	Company Book for Co. of Lt. George N. Morris and Capt. John R. Bell, Light Art. 1814-15.

Volumes	Title
171	Company Book for Co. of Capt. William F. Hobart, Light Art. 1818-21.
172	Company Book for Co. of Capt. William F. Hobart, Light Art. 1817-18.
173	Company Book for Co. of Capt. Henry Knox Craig, Light Art. 1815-17.
174	Company Book for Co. of Capt. Henry Knox Craig, Light Art. 1818-21.
175	Clothing Book for Co. of Capts. John Ritchie and Alexander C. W. Fanning, 2d Art. 1812-15.
176	Company Book for Co. of Capt. Horace H. Watson, 3d Art. 1812-17.
177	Company Book for Co. of Capt. James House, 1st Art. 1806-11.
178	Company Book for Co. of Capt. James N. Barker, 2d Art. 1812-15.
179	Company Book for Co. of Capt. James T. B. Romayne, 3d Art. 1812-16.
180	Company Book for Co. of Capt. James R. Hanham, Corps of Art. 1814-15.
181	Company Book for Co. of Capt. William Van Deursen, 3d Art. 1812-14.
182	Company Book for Co. of Capt. Alexander J. Williams, 2d Art. 1813-15.
183	Company Book for Co. of Capt. Moses Swett, 2d Art. 1812-15.
184	Company Book for Co. of Capt. Thomas Bennett, 1st Art. 1810-15.
185*	"Capt. Jas. Green Jr's Co. Art. 1813-15." (Not found)
186	Company Book for Co. of Capts. John Ritchie and Alexander C. W. Fanning, 2d Art. 1812-14.
187	Company Book for Co. of Capt. James Reed, 1st Art. 1812-15.
188	Company Book for Co. of Capt. Benjamin K. Pierce, 3d Art. 1813-15.
189	Company Book for Co. of Capt. James N. Barker, 2d Art. 1815.
190	Company Book for Co. of Capt. Alexander C. W. Fanning, 3d Art. 1812-15.
191	Clothing Book for Co. of Capts. Alexander C. W. Fanning and Roger Jones, 3d Art. 1812-15.
192	Company Book for Co. of Capt. Rufus McIntire, 3d Art. 1812-15.
193*	"Capt. Wm. Gates' Co. Art. 1815." (Not found)
194	Company Book for Co. of Capt. Julius F. Heileman, 1st Art. 1813-15.
195	Company Book for Co. of Capt. James H. Boyles, Corps of Art. 1814-15.

Volumes	Title
196	Company Book for Co. of Capt. Richard A. Zantzinger and Lt. Robert Stewart, Corps of Art. 1814-15.
197	Company Book for Co. of Capt. Ichabod B. Crane, 3d Art. 1812-15.
198	Company Book for Co. of Capts. Lowndes Brown and Greenleaf Dearborn, Corps of Art. 1818-21.
199	Company Book for Co. of Capt. Edward Wadsworth, 1st Rifles. 1812-15.
200	Company Book for Co. of Capt. William Smyth and Lt. Samuel Hamilton, 1st Rifles. 1813-15.
201	Company Book for Co. of Capt. George Gray, 1st Rifles, 1812-15.
202	Company Book for Co. of Capt. Thomas Ramsey, 1st Rifles. 1814-15.
203	Company Book for Co. of Capts. Alexander W. Brandon and William C. Parker, 3d Rifles. 1814-15.
204	Company Book for Co. of Capt. Wyly Martin, 3d Rifles. 1814-15.
205	Muster and Receipt Rolls for Co. of Capts. Thomas J. Robeson and Walter Coles, 3d Rifles. 1814-15.
206	Company Book for Co. of Capts. John G. Blount and William Dufphey, 3d Rifles. 1814-15.
207	Company Book for Co. of Capts. John E. Calhoun and Walter Coles, 3d Rifles. 1814-15.
208	Company Book for Co. of Capts. James Dorman and John Jamison, 5th Inf. 1814-15.
209	Company Book for Co. of Capt. Richard H. Bell, 5th Inf. 1810-14.
210	Company Book for Co. of Capt. James Masters, 6th Inf. 1811-15.
211	Company Book for Co. of Capt. John Chapman, 6th Inf. 1814-15.
212	Company Book for Co. of Capts. Gad Humphreys and James Bailey, 6th Inf. 1813-15.
213	Company Book for Co. of Capt. Walter H. Overton, 7th Inf. 1811-15.
214	Company Book for Co. of Capt. James Doherty, 7th Inf. 1813-15.
215	Company Book for Co. of Capts. John N. McIntosh and Lewis B. Willis, 8th Inf. 1819-21.
216	Company Book for a Detachment Under Capt. William Davenport, 8th Inf. 1818-21.
217	Company Book for Co. of Capt. Lewis B. Willis, 8th Inf. 1819-21.
218	Descriptive List of Capt. Chester Lyman's Co., 9th Inf. 1812-13.

Volumes	Title
219	Company Book for Co. of Capts. George Bender and Samuel Allen, 9th Inf. 1813-15.
220	Company Book for Co. of Capts. Abraham F. Hull and Moses Hoit, 9th Inf. 1812-15.
221	Company Book for Co. of Capt. Abraham F. Hull, 9th Inf. 1814.
222	Company Book for Co. of Capt. William L. Foster, 9th Inf. 1814.
223	Company Book for Co. of Capt. Horatio Stark, 1st Inf. 1812-15.
224	Company Book for Co. of Lt. Daniel Chandler, 9th Inf. 1814-15.
225	Company Book for Co. of Capt. George Vashon, 10th Inf. 1813-15.
226	Company Book for Co. of Capt. John Whistler, 1st Inf. 1811-12.
227	Company Book for Co. of Capt. John W. Weeks, 11th Inf. 1812-14.
228	Company Book for Co. of Capts. John W. Weeks and Malachi Corning, 11th Inf. 1814.
229	Company Book for Co. of Capts. Joseph Griswold and William S. Foster, 11th Inf. 1812-15.
230	Company Book for Co. of Capt. Benjamin Smead, 11th Inf. 1812-15.
231	Company Book for Co. of Capt. John Bliss, 11th Inf. 1813-14.
232	Company Book for Co. of Capts. Valentine R. Goodrich and John Bliss, 11th Inf. 1812-14.
233	Company Book for Co. of Capt. John Bliss, 11th Inf. 1813-14.
234	Company Book for Co. of Capts. Richard Bean and Malachi Corning, 11th Inf. 1813-14.
235	Company Book for Co. of Capt. William S. Foster, 11th Inf. 1814-15.
236	Company Book for Co. of Capt. Thomas Post, 12th Inf. 1813-15.
237	Clothing Book for Co. of Capt. Thomas Post, 12th Inf. 1814-15.
238	Company Book for Co. of Capt. Thomas Biddle, Corps of Art. 1818-21.
239	Company Book for Co. of Capt. James Paxton, 12th Inf. 1812-15.
240	Company Book for Co. of Capts. James Charlton and Thomas Sangster, 12th Inf. 1813-15.
241	Company Book for Co. of Capt. Thomas Sangster, 12th Inf. 1815.
242	Company Book for Co. of Capt. Andrew L. Madison, 12th Inf. 1812-15.
243	Orderly Book for Co. of Capt. A. L. Madison, 12th Inf. 1813-14.
244	Company Book for Co. of Capt. Thomas P. Moore, 12th Inf. 1813-14.

Volumes	Title

245   Company Book for Co. of Capt. Lewis B. Willis, 12th Inf.
        1814-15.

246   Company Book for Co. of Capt. Myndert M. Dox, 13th Inf.
        1813-15.

247   Company Book for Co. of Capt. William B. Adams, 13th Inf.
        1814-15.

248   Company Book for Co. of Capt. John K. Paige, 13th Inf.
        1813-15.

249   Company Book for Co. of Capt. Mordecai Meyer, 13th Inf.
        1814-15.

250*   "Capt. J. D. Finks' Co. 13th Inf. 1814-15."(Not found)

251   Company Book for Co. of Capt. Stephen W. Kearny, 13th Inf.
        1814.

252   Company Book for Co. of Capt. Stephen W. Kearny, 13th Inf.
        1814-15.

253   Company Book for Co. of Capt. Samuel Lane, 14th Inf. 1812-15.

254*   "Capt. Robert Gray and J. F. McElroys' Co. 16th Inf."
        (Not found)

255   Company Book for Co. of Capt. James F. McElroy, 16th Inf.
        1814-15.

256   Company Book for Co. of Capt. William Davenport, 16th Inf.
        1813-14.

257   Company Book for Co. of Capt. William Davenport, 16th Inf.
        1814-15.

258   Company Book for Co. of Lt. Thomas M. Powers, 16th Inf.
        1813-15.

259   Company Book for Co. of Capt. Nathaniel McLaughlin, 16th Inf.
        1814-15.

260   Company Book for Co. of Capts. John Baldy and Thomas Horrell,
        16th Inf. 1814-15.

261   Company Book for Co. of Capts. Jonathan Aitken and Thomas
        Horrell, 16th Inf. 1814-15.

262   Company Book for Co. of Capts. John Stanard and John Macrae,
        20th Inf. 1812-14.

263   Company Book for Co. of Capt. Byrd C. Willis, 20th Inf.
        1813-14.

264   Company Book for Co. of Capt. William S. Jett, 20th Inf.
        1812-14.

265   Company Book for Co. of Capt. Lemuel Bradford, 21st Inf.
        1812-14.

266   Company Book for Co. of Capt. Morrill Marston, 21st Inf.
        1813-14.

Volumes	Title
267	Letters and Orders of Capt. Jeremiah Chapman, 21st Inf., Commanding the Recruiting District Under the Boston Rendezvous. 1812-13.
268	Company Book for Co. of Capt. Sullivan Burbank, 21st Inf. 1814.
269	Company Book for Co. of Capt. Charles Procter, 21st Inf. 1813-15.
270	Company Book for Co. of Capt. Joseph Treat, 21st Inf. 1813-15.
271	Company Book for Co. of Capt. Lemuel Bradford, 21st Inf. 1814-15.
272	Company Book for Co. of Capts. Lemuel Bradford and Ira Drew, 21st Inf. 1814-15.
273	Company Book for Co. of Capt. John Pentland, 22d Inf. 1812-14.
274	Company Book for Co. of Capt. John Pentland, 22d Inf. 1814.
275	Company Book for Co. of Capt. George W. Barker and Lt. Thomas Y. Sprogell, 22d Inf. 1813.
276	Company Book for Co. of Capts. David Milliken and Daniel McFarland, 22d Inf. 1812-13.
277	Company Book for Co. of Capt. Willis Foulk, 22d Inf. 1813-15.
278	Company Book for Co. of Capt. Thomas Lawrence, 22d Inf. 1814.
279	Company Book for Co. of Capt. Thomas Lawrence, 22d Inf. 1814-15.
280	Company Book for Co. of Capt. Joseph Henderson, 22d Inf. 1813-15.
281	Company Book for Co. of Capt. Jacob Carmack, 22d Inf. 1814-15.
282	Company Book for Co. of Lt. Justus Ingersoll, 23d Inf. 1814-15.
283	Company Book for Co. of Capt. Richard Goodell, 23d Inf. 1814.
284	Company Book for Co. of Capt. Frederick Brown, 23d Inf. 1814-15.
285	Company Book for Co. of Capts. Azariah W. Odell and Lt. William Belknap, 23d Inf. 1814-15.
286	Company Book for Co. of Capt. George Howard, 25th Inf. 1812-13.
287	Company Book for Co. of Capt. Thomas S. Seymour, 25th Inf. 1814-15.
288	Company Book for Co. of Capts. Festus Cone and Thomas M. Read, 25th Inf. 1812-14.
289	Register of Clothing, Arms, and Ammunition Issued to Co. of Capts. Benjamin Watson and James Burbidge, 25th Inf. 1814-15.
290	Company Book for Co. of Capt. Edward White, 25th Inf. 1814-15.
291	Company Book for Co. of Capt. Peter Bradley, 25th Inf. 1813-14.
292	Company Book for Co. of Capts. Jesse Beach and Daniel Ketchum, 25th Inf. 1814.

Volumes	Title
293	Company Book for Co. of Capt. Archibald C. Crary, 25th Inf. 1814-15.
294	Company Book for Co. of Capts. Jesse Beach and Daniel Ketchum, 25th Inf. 1814-15.
295	Company Book for Co. of Capt. Elijah Boardman, 26th Inf. 1814-15.
296	Company Book for Co. of Capts. John Levake and Salmon C. Cotton. 26th Inf. 1814-15.
297	Company Book for Co. of Capt. Ira Williams, 26th Inf. 1814-15.
298	Company Book for Co. of Capt. Aaron T. Crane, 27th Inf. 1814-15.
299	Orderly Book and Company Book for Co. of Capt. Christian Hartell, 27th Inf. 1814-15.
300	Company Book for Co. of Capt. Thomas Earle, 27th Inf. 1814-15.
301	Company Book for Co. of Capt. James Porter, 27th Inf. 1814-15.
302	Company Book for Co. of Capt. Allen Reynolds, 27th Inf. 1814-15.
303	Company Book for Co. of Capt. Benjamin F. Wood, 27th Inf. 1814-15.
304	Company Book for Co. of Capt. James B. Spencer, 29th Inf. 1814-15.
305	Company Book for Co. of Capt. John C. Rochester, 29th Inf. 1813-15.
306	Company Book for Co. of Capt. Peter B. Van Buren, 29th Inf. 1813-15.
307	Company Book for Co. of Capt. William Miller, 30th Inf. 1813-15.
308	Company Book for Co. of Capt. David Sanford, 30th Inf. 1814-15.
309	Company Book for Co. of Capt. James Taylor, 30th Inf. 1815.
310	Company Book for Co. of Capt. Ethan Burnap, 31st Inf. 1814-15.
311	Company Book for Co. of Capt. Rufus Stewart, 31st Inf. 1814-15.
312	Company Book for Co. of Capt. Andrew Arnold, 31st Inf. 1814-15.
313	Company Book for Co. of Capt. Samuel Borden, 32d Inf. 1813-15.
314	Company Book for Co. of Capt. John Steele, Jr., 32d Inf. 1814-15.
315	Orderly Book and Company Book for Co. of Capt. George F. Goodman, 32nd Inf. 1814-15.
316	Company Book for Co. of Capt. Benjamin Dunn, 33d Inf. 1814-15.
317	Company Book for Co. of Capt. James Curry, 33d Inf. 1814-15.

Volumes	Title
318	Company Book for Co. of Capt. Robert R. Ke Jall, 34th Inf. 1814-15.
319	Company Book for Co. of Capt. Peter Chadwic , 34th Inf. 1814-15.
320	Company Book for Co. of Capt. Thomas Bailey, 34th Inf. 1814-15.
321	Company Book for Co. of Capt. Isaac Carter, 4th Inf. 1814-15.
322	Company Book for Co. of Capt. Benjamin Poland 34th Inf. 1814-15.
323	Company Book for Co. of Capt. Walter T. Cocke, 35th Inf. 1814-15.
324	Company Book for Co. of Capt. Francis E. Walke: . 35th Inf. 1814-15.
325	Company Book for Co. of Capt. Christopher Riple , 37th Inf. 1813-15.
326	Company Book for Co. of Capt. Elizur Warner, 37 h Inf. 1813-15.
327	Company Book for Co. of Capt. Stephen D. Tilden, 37th Inf. 1814-15.
328	Company Book for Co. of Capt. Samuel B. Northrop, 37th Inf. 1813-15.
329	Company Book for Co. of Capt. John Brown, 37th Inf. 1814-15.
330	Company Book for Co. of Capts. Chauncey Ives and David T. Welch, 37th Inf. 1813-15.
331	Company Book for Co. of Capt. Leonard Ross, 30th Inf. 1813-14.
332	Company Book for Co. of Capt. Mathew N. Sandborn and Lt. William B. Parker, 40th Inf. 1814-15.
333	Company Book for Co. of Capt. Robert Neale, 40th Inf. 1813-14.
334	Descriptive Rolls of Recruits Enlisted by Capt. Jacob B. Varnum and Other Officers, 40th Inf. 1813-15.
335	Company Book for Co. of Capt. Alpheus Sherman, 41st Inf. 1814-15.
336	Company Book for Co. of Capt. Charles Humphrey, 41st Inf. 1814-15.
337	Company Book for Co. of Capts. Samuel Berrian and John Ingersoll, 41st Inf. 1813-15.
338	Company Book for Co. of Capt. William S. Radcliff, 41st Inf. 1814-15.
339	Company Book for Co. of Capt. Gilbert Seaman, 41st Inf. 1814-15.
340	Company Book for Co. of Capt. Francis Allyn, 41st Inf. 1813-15.
341	Company Book for Co. of Capt. Mangle M. Quackenbos, 41st Inf. 1814-15.
342	Company Book for Co. of Capt. James F. De Peyster, 42d Inf. 1814-15.

Volumes	Title

343   Company Book for Co. of Capt. Edmund B. Duval, 42d Inf. 1814-15.

344   Company Book for Co. of Capt. George W. Barker, 42d Inf. 1814-15.

345   Company Book for Co. of Capts. John Biddle and Thomas Hanson, 42d Inf. 1814-15.

346   Company Book for Co. of Capt. John Biddle, 42d Inf. 1813-15.

347*   "Capt. Thos. Hanson's Co. 42d Inf. 1814-15." (Not found)

348   Company Book for Co. of Capt. George Dabney, 43d Inf. 1814-15.

349   Company Book for Co. of Capt. Daniel M. Gregg, 45th Inf. 1814-15.

350   Morning Reports for the Bn. at Greenbush and Plattsburg, N.Y., Light Art. 1815.

351   Morning Reports for the Bn. at Greenbush and Plattsburg, N.Y., Light Art., 1815-16; Morning Reports for the Bn. Forming the Garrison at Fort Independence, Light Art., 1818-19.

352   Morning Reports for the Bn. Forming the Garrison at Fort Independence, Boston Harbor, Light Art. 1817-18.

353   Morning Reports for the Bn. Forming the Garrison at Fort Independence, Boston Harbor, Light Art. 1818.

354   Morning Reports for the Bn. Forming the Garrison at Fort Independence, Boston Harbor, Light Art. 1819-20.

355   Morning Reports, 7th Inf. 1811-12; 1814.

356*   Army Register, Inspector General's Office. 1812-13. (In RG94)

357   Company Returns, Inspector General, 3d Mil. Dist. 1814.

358   Reports Sent by Inspector General, 4th and 10th Mil. Dist. 1815.

359*   Reports of Ordnance Equipment and Stores, 1812. (In RG156)

360   Provision Returns, Garrison of New Orleans. 1809-16.

361   Reports of Strength and Details for Guard Duty, Garrison of New Orleans, 7th Inf. 1812-15.

362   Company Book for Co. of Capt. James Doherty, 7th Inf. 1808-11.

363   Morning Reports, Light Art. 1814-15.

364   Company Book for Co. of Capt. Josiah H. Vose, 21st Inf. 1813-14.

365   Company Book for Co. of Capt. William N. Irvine, Light Art. 1808-9.

366   Letters and Orders, Col. John Breck, Commanding Fort Independence. 1815.

367   Orderly Book for Co. of Capt. William L. Cooper, 1st Art. 1803-4.

368   Orderly Book of the Adjutant, Garrison of New Orleans. 1807-8.

369   Orderly Book of the Adjutant, Garrison of New Orleans. 1812-13.

370   Orderly Book of an Unidentified Co., 7th Inf. 1812.

Volumes	Title
371	Orderly Book of an Unidentified Co., 7th Inf. 1812.
372	Orderly Book for Co. of Capt. Richard Oldham, 7th Inf. 1812.
373	Orderly Book for an Unidentified Co., 7th Inf. 1812-13.
374	Orderly Book for an Unidentified Co., 7th Inf. 1813.
375	Orderly Book for a Detachment Under Capt. William McClellan, 7th Inf. 1813-14.
376	Orderly Book for an Unidentified Co., 7th Inf. 1813-14.
377	Morning Reports, 7th Inf. 1814-15.
378	Orderly Book, 7th Inf. 1815.
379	Morning Reports, 7th Inf. 1815.
380	Orderly Book, 7th Inf. 1820-21.
381	Orderly Book, 8th Inf. 1820-21.
382*	General Orders Issued by Brig. Gen. James Wilkinson. 1797-1808. (In RG 94; undoubtedly first third of first volume described in entry 44, Preliminary Inventory 17)
383	Orderly Book of the Adjutant, District Commander, Maj. Gen. Charles C. Pinckney. 1800.
384-385*	General Orders Issued by Brig. Gen. James Wilkinson. 1797-1808. (In RG 94; undoubtedly the last two parts of the first volume described in entry 44, Preliminary Inventory 17)
386	Orders and Muster Reports, Sabine Expedition. 1806-7.
387	Orderly Book for Co. of Capts. Mossman Houston and William R. Davis, 3d Inf. in Maj. Z. M. Pike's Consolidated Regt. 1809-10.
388	Orderly Book for Adjutant, Maj. Z. M. Pike's Consolidated Regt. 1810.
389	Orderly Book of the Adjutant, 3d Mil. Dist. 1812-14.
390	Orderly Book of the Adjutant at Sackett's Harbor, 9th Mil. Dist. 1812-13.
391	Orderly Book of the Adjutant, 7th Mil. Dist. and Div. of the South. 1813-16.
392*	Letters of the Quartermaster General. 1797. (In RG92)
393	Letters and Orders, 4th Mil. Dist. 1813-14.
394	Second Brigade Orders, 9th Mil. Dist. 1813.
395	Fourth Brigade Orders, 9th Mil. Dist. 1813.
396	Orders, Adjutant at French Mills, 2d Div., 9th Mil. Dist. 1813-14.
397	Orderly Book, 3d Art. 1813.
398*	"Orders, 8th Mil. Dist. and Div. South, 1814-16."(Not found)
399*	"Orders, 1st Inf., Baton Rouge, 1817." (Not found)
400	Orderly Book for Co. of Capt. Robert L. Coomb, 1st Inf. 1820-21.
401	Letters Received by Maj. Thomas Cushing, Commanding Troops on the Mississippi. 1799.

Volumes	Title
402	Letters Sent by Maj. Thomas Cushing, Commanding Troops on the Mississippi. 1799-1800.
403*	Letters, Acting Inspector General. 1812. (In RG94)
404*	"Letters, Gen. Hull at Detroit, Gen. Dearborn at Albany, 1812." (Not found)
405	Letters and Circulars, Right Wing. 9th Mil. Dist. 1814-15.
406	Letters, Inspector General, 9th Mil. Dist. 1814-15.
407	Letters, Div. of the South. 1816-21.
408	Letters, 5th Mil. Dept. 1817-21.
409	Letters, Div. of the North. 1818-21.
410-416*	Letters, Inspector's Office, Washington. 1800-1809. (In RG94)
417*	Letters Relating to Supts. of Indian Trading Houses. 1800. (In RG75)
418*	Minutes of the Council With the Choctaws at Hobukintopa. 1805. (In RG75)
419*	Register of Officers in Recruiting Service. ca. 1814. (In RG94)
420*	Returns of the North Carolina Militia, 1813. (In RG94)
421*	"Ordnance Report, 1799-1800." (Not found)
422*	List of Applications for Appointments in the Volunteer Army. n.d. (In RG94)
423	List of Officers Reporting, 3d Mil. Dist. 1813-14.
424	Register of Officers, 9th Mil. Dist. 1814-15.
425	Morning Reports, 7th Inf. 1813-14.
426*	Monthly Returns of the British Garrison at Fort George. 1809-12. (In RG94)
427	Register of Officers, Div. of the North. 1815.
428	Orderly Book, 7th Inf. 1813-14.
429	Orderly Book for the First Light Co., 7th Inf. 1817-18.
430	Orderly Book for Co. of Capt. John Darrington, 3d Inf., in Maj. Z. M. Pike's Consolidated Regt. 1811.
431	Orderly Book Probably for Co. of Capt. Matthew Arbuckle, Camp Natchitoches, La., 2d Inf. 1804-5.
432	Orderly Book for Co. of Capt. William Butler Detailed Under Capt. Richard Call, 1st Inf. 1816-17.
433	Orderly Book of the Adjutant, 7th Mil. Dist. 1813-14.
434	Orderly Book for the Co. of Capt. Joseph Miles, 1st Inf. 1817.
435	Orderly Book of the Adjutant, 8th Mil. Dept. 1817-20.
436	Orderly Book for Co. of Capt. William Laval Detailed Under Capt. Robert Coomb, 1st Inf. 1816.
437	Orderly Book, Garrison of New Orleans. 1809.
438	Orderly Book for an Unidentified Co., 3d Inf. 1814.
439	Orderly Book of a Rifle Detachment, Northern Army, 9th Mil. Dist. 1813-15.

Volumes	Title
440	Orderly Book of the Adjutant, Sackett's Harbor, 9th Mil. Dist. 1814.
441	Orderly Book, Brigade Inspector's Office, 5th Mil. Dept. 1816-17.
442	Orderly Book of the Adjutant, Northern Army, 9th Mil. Dist. 1814.
443	Orderly Book, Brigade Inspector's Office, 5th Mil. Dept. 1817-18.
444	Orderly Book, Co. H., Light Art. 1817-18.
445	Orderly Book of the Adjutant, Northern Army, 9th Mil. Dist. 1813-14.
446	Orderly Book of the Adjutant, Sackett's Harbor, 9th Mil. Dist. 1814.
447	Orderly Book of the Inspector, Northern Dept. 1812-13.
448	Orderly Book, Co. H, Light Art. 1816-17.
449	Orderly Book of the Adjutant, 3d Mil. Dist. 1816-18.
450	War Dept., Div. of the South, and 8th Mil. Dept. Orders, 1st Inf. 1816-19.
451	Orderly Book of the Inspector, 3d Mil. Dist. 1815.
452	Brigade Orders, 2d Div., Northern Army, 9th Mil. Dist. 1814.
453	General Orders, Adjutant and Inspector, 4th and 10th Mil. Dist. 1815.
454	Orderly Book of the Adjutant, 7th Mil. Dist. 1814-15.
455	General Orders, Northern Army, 9th Mil. Dist. 1814.
456	Orderly Book of the Inspector, Northern Army, 9th Mil. Dist. 1814-15.
457	Orderly Book of the Adjutant, Sackett's Harbor, 9th Mil. Dist. 1815.
458	Orderly Book of the Inspector, 3d Mil. Dist. 1812-14.
459*	"Orders, 4th and 10th Mil. Dist., Baltimore, 1814-15." (Not found)
460	Orderly Book, 4th Mil. Dist. and Dept. 1814-19.
461	General Orders, 3d Mil. Dist. and Dept. 1814-18.
462	Orderly Book of the Bn., Fort Independence, Light Art. 1818-19.
463	Orderly Book, 5th Mil. Dept. 1818-21.
464	Orderly Book of the Adjutant, Northern Army, 9th Mil. Dist. 1814.
465	Orderly Book of the Adjutant, Northern Army, 9th Mil. Dist. 1814-15.
466	Orderly Book of the Adjutant, 3d Mil. Dist. 1814-16.
467*	"Not on file." (Not found)
468	Orderly Book, 5th Mil. Dept. 1818-20.
469	Orderly Book for the Co. of Capt. Anatole Peychaud, 1st Inf. 1817-18.

Volumes	Title
470	Orderly Book, 1st and 3d Mil. Depts. 1818-21.
471	Orderly Book for Co. of Capt. William Lawrence, 2d Inf. 1813.
472	Orderly Book, Garrison of New Orleans. 1808-9.
473	Orderly Book of an Unidentified Co., 3d Inf. 1815.
474	Orderly Book for Co. of Capt. Joseph Dinkins, 3d Inf. 1812-14.
475	Orderly Book for Co. of Capt. William Lawrence, 2d Inf. 1809-11.
476	Orderly Book for Co. of Capt. Ferdinand Amelung, 1st Inf. 1821-22.
477*	"Orders, Baton Rouge, 1811." (Not found)
478	Orderly Book for an Unidentified Co., 1st Inf. 1816.
479	Orderly Book for Co. of Capt. William Christian, 1st Inf. 1815.
480	Orderly Book for Co. of Capt. John Steele, 3d Inf. 1799.
481	Orderly Book for an Unidentified Co., 1st Inf. 1815-16.
482	Orderly Book for Co. of Capt. Amos Stoddard, 1st Art. 1807-8.
483	Orderly Book for Co. of Capt. William Laval, 1st Inf. 1819-20.
484	Orderly Book of the Brigade Major, 8th Mil. Dept. 1815-16.
485	Orderly Book for Co. of Capt. William Lawrence, 2d Inf. 1811-12.
486	Orderly Book for Co. of Capt. Samuel Vail, 7th Inf. 1814-15.
487	Orderly Book, Garrison of New Orleans. 1806.
488	Orderly Book, Garrison of New Orleans. 1810-12.
489	Orderly Book for Co. of Capt. Ferdinand Amelung, 1st Inf. 1817-18.
490	Orderly Book for an Unidentified Co., 2d Inf. 1813-14.
491	Orderly Book, Division of the North. 1815-20.
492	Orderly Book, Brigade Inspector, 5th Mil. Dept. 1815.
493	Orderly Book, Co. H, Light Art. 1815-17.
494	Orderly Book, Brigade Inspector, 5th Mil. Dept. 1815-16.
495	General Orders, Maj. Gen. Wade Hampton, 9th Mil. Dist. 1813.
496	Orderly Book for an Unidentified Co., 3d Inf. 1814-15.
497	Orderly Book for Co. of Capt. Thomas Hunter, 3d Inf. 1815.
498	Orderly Book for Co. of Capt. Joseph Dinkins, 3d Inf. 1812.
499	Orders, Legion. 1792-93.
500	Orderly Book for Co. of Capt. Isaac Baker, 1st Inf. 1815-16.
501	Orderly Book for Co. of Capt. Thomas Ramsey, 1st Rifles. 1813-15.
502	Orderly Book for Co. of Capt. Isaac Baker, 1st Inf. 1817.
503	Orderly Book for Co. of Capt. James E. Dinkins, 3d Inf., in Maj. Z. M. Pike's Consolidated Regt. 1811.
504	Orderly Book for a Detachment of Co. of Capt. Joseph Bowmar, 2d Inf., 1806; Orderly Book for an Unidentified Co., 2d Inf., 1807.

Volumes	Title

505   Orderly Book for an Unidentified Co , 1st Inf. 1815-16.
506   Orderly Book, Second Brigade, 9th Mil. Dist. 1813.
507   Orders of the Adjutant, Sackett's Harbor, 9th Mil. Dist.
       1813.
508   Orders, Adjutant and Inspector, Northern Army, 9th Mil.
       Dist. 1814.
509   Orders, Adjutant and Inspector, Northern Army, 9th Mil.
       Dist. 1814.
510*   "Orders, Guard Details, Northern Army 1814." (Not found)
511   Detail Orders, 10th Mil. Dist. 1814.
512   Letters and Orders, Gen. Edmund Gaine , 9th Mil. Dist. 1814.
513   Register of Men and Officers Detailed Left Div., Northern
       Army, 9th Mil. Dist. 1814.
514   Receipts for Blank Forms, 3d Mil. Dis . 1814.
515   Morning Reports, 8th Inf. 1821.
516*   Register of Blanks and Books Distributed Since June 1821.
       (In RG94)
517   Orderly Book of the Bn., Fort Independence, Light Art.
       1819-20.
518   Orderly Book, Div. of the North. 1820-21.
519-527*   "Not on file." (Not found)
528   Monthly Returns, 1st Art. 1807-11.
529*   Monthly Roll of the 49th British Inf. 1798. (In RG94)
530*   Orderly Book, British Horse Guards. 1812. (In RG94)
531*   Account Book, Co. G., 49th British Inf. 1811-12. (In RG94)
532-549*   (Crossed out by AGO)
550   Register of Men Discharged, 9th Mil. Dist. 1814-15.
551   Register of Men Discharged, 3d Mil. Dist. 1813-15.
552   Register of Patients in Hospital, 9th Mil. Dist. 1814-15.
553   Register of Men Discharged, 3d Mil. Dist. 1812-15.
554   Register of Men Discharged, 3d Mil. Dist. 1816-19.
555   Register of Men Discharged, 9th Mil. Dist. 1815.
556   Register of Men Discharged, 9th Mil. Dist. 1814-15.
557*   Company Book for Officers and Privates, Ordnance Dept.
       1814-19. (In RG156)
558   Register of Men Discharged, 5th Mil. Dept. 1815-17.
559*   (No number assigned)
560   Register of Men Discharged, 5th Mil. Dept. 1815-21.
561   Register of Men Discharged, 9th Mil. Dist. 1814-15.
562   Register of Men Discharged, 9th Mil. Dist. 1812-15.
563   Lists of Discharges, Desertions, and Deaths, 4th Mil. Dist.
       1813-14.
564*   "Discharges of Pensioners, Invalids, and Militia, 1814-15."
       (Not found)

Volumes	Title

565* "Co. Book. U.S. Art., 1815-19." (Not found)

566 List of Soldiers Who Died at Hospitals, 9th Mil. Dist. 1813-16.

567* "Hospital Returns, 1814-15." (Not found)

568* "Discharges: Invalids, 1815-16." (Not found)

569 Register of Men Furloughed and Discharged, 1st Mil. Dist. 1813-15.

570* "Deaths, Discharges and Substitutes, 1815-23." (Not found)

571-572* (No numbers assigned)

573* "Desertions, U.S. Army, 1815-23." (Not found)

574-662* Muster Rolls. (In RG94)

663-674* Bounty Books. (In RG94)

675 Letters, 6th Mil. Dist. 1813-15.

676* "Capts.Mulford and Wilson's Co. Bk, Art. 1811-13."(Not found)

677 General Orders and Orders, Southern Dept. 1812-13.

678 General Orders and Orders, Southern Dept. 1812.

679 Letters, 6th Mil. Dist. 1813.

680 Register of Patients in the Hospital, 9th Mil. Dist. 1814.

681 Orderly Book of the Adjutant, 6th Mil. Dist. 1815.

682 Orderly Book of the Adjutant, 6th Mil. Dist. 1813-14.

683 Register of Patients in the Hospital, 9th Mil. Dist. 1814-15.

684 Company Book for Co. of Capt. Robert Fenner, 18th Inf. 1814-15.

685 Letters and Orders, 4th Inf. 1811-12; Returns, 41st Inf. 1813.

686* (No number assigned)

687* "Army Register, 1792-1812." (Not found)

688 Orderly and Company Book for Co. of Capt. Benjamin K. Pierce, Corps of Art., 1815-18.

689* Important General Orders and Other Orders Issued by Northern Army, 1812-14 (typed copies). (In RG94)

B. List of 27 Unnumbered Volumes

Title

Orderly Book for Garrison at Castle Island, Boston Harbor. 1786-87. (Entry 9).

Records of the Garrison at Fort Independence, Boston Harbor. 1803-15. (Entry 10).

Orderly Book for the Garrison at Fort Johnston, N.C. 1795-1811. (Entry 12).

Guard Details and Rosters of Officers. 1795. (Entry 16).

Letters, Daniel D. Tompkins, Gov. of N.Y. 1812-14. (Entry 19).

www.ingramcontent.com/pod-product-compliance
Lightning Source LLC
LaVergne TN
LVHW081320060426
835509LV00015B/1605